NAVIGATING LIFE'S CHANGES AFTER HIGH SCHOOL: SUCCESS GUIDE

Debraca Russell MBA CPCC

Contributing Authors:

Allison Haviland

Javed Morgan

Zaneta Ellison LMHC

Special thanks go out to the students who graciously
modeled for the cover of this book:
Chainey, Darvin, Max and Riselle.

DENISE THOMAS, EDITOR & FOUNDER OF CARVED OUT DIVAS MENTORSHIP PROGRAM

Denise Thomas, I thank you for not quitting after 5 million edits for this resource guide. Your patience and resilience have been instrumental in creating such a solid book. You understood the importance of getting it right the first time. You are truly appreciated!

As a teacher and a community advocate Denise is always making her voice heard by better things around her. When Denise is not teaching her middle school students, she is mentoring her group of young ladies known as Carved Out Divas. This mentorship program was created for girls to show them how to function in various social settings. The girls in this program are mentored with etiquette classes, career planning, speech classes, confidence building workshops, financial planning, and tons of girl time drinking tea! When Denise is not mentoring, she is traveling the world creating memories. Denise can be reached at the below mentioned contact details.

Email: denise@carvedoutdivas.com
Website: https://carvedoutdivas.com/
Facebook: https://www.facebook.com/CarvedOutDivas/
Instagram: https://www.instagram.com/carvedoutdivas/

Mailing Address:
Carved Out Divas
P.O. Box 310667
Tampa, Florida, United States
(813) 699-0887

FOREWORD

Life, Oh the uncertainties. The twists and the turns, the unexpected, with so many transitions. I remember graduating from high school like it was yesterday. Being prepared for my next steps in life, took a lot of work on my part and support from my parents, especially my Mom. "Transitioning Your Life After High School: Success Guide" is an essential book for students, parents, and guardians.

This book will prepare students for graduation including moving to a new city or state, finding a place to live and job searches. Knowing and learning how to process what you are feeling in the midst of a transition is critical and this book will give multiple ideas to help young adults do just that. Educating your teen about making their step into independence and adulthood can prove to be scary. One author, a Licensed Mental Health Counselor, lays out how life transitions effect all people in different ways. She explains how your teen and their guardian can navigate through mental and emotional coping as the transition process occurs.

The main take away of this book is how it provides soon to be graduating students several options of paths they can pursue after high school. Being a public-school teacher, I know that each student is created uniquely and is passionate about different things. This book graciously encourages students to explore multiple avenues where they may find their distinct fit. Encouraging your student to walk in their truth towards their destiny is the key this book consistently mentions.

I remember growing up, with everyone saying college is the only way to go. This phobia is saddening to me. I believe college is a great next step, but it is not the only step. Your teen can choose various positive paths after high school and all of them would be considered smart. College does not make you the wiser. Life experiences and learning through living is what makes us wiser. This book encourages parents and guardians to allow their teen to speak their desires and follow their aspirations removing the stigma behind choices.

.I love how one author, a financial aid advisor, lays out steps to help your teen stay out of debt or have very minimal debt if you choose the college route by explaining the differences between federal scholarships and federal loan options. Scholarship search tools are also a priceless commodity explained in this guide. It talks of the importance of planning during your scholarship search by setting aside time to fill out scholarship applications. Scholarships and grants are how you avoid mounting and looming debt. Another topic bridged by this book is professional career advice that highlights how internships and apprenticeship programs can allow your teen to test the waters of a career without committing their whole life to it.

The last author, a financial planner, explains how managing money, budgeting, and paying off any debt are lessons your teen will need today, tomorrow, and forever. This helpful guide will assist you and your teen reach their goals. Believe me, you want to get your copy because the commitment required to read this book, is worth every minute invested.

Amber Martin, Educator

WHAT QUALIFIES ME TO WRITE THIS BOOK? THE CHOICE TO BUILD MY LEGACY.

I have always been outspoken, unpredictable, out of control, keep you guessing, what did she do again, unruly Russell child that makes others cringe. I decided to use all the negative words spoken to me and about me, my decisions, and my mistakes to build a platform of determination. Determination to live life with no regrets, should haves, or maybes. When you ask me, "What qualifies me to write this book", my answer is, I survived and I am thriving. My name is Debraca Sivongile Russell, the statistic that refused to settle for what I was born in or raised in.

Bastard, accident, or anchor baby; whatever term you chose, I was not a planned pregnancy, a planned college graduate, nor was I a planned entrepreneur. If you fast forward 30 something years later, my statistics I assure you, are still chart worthy.

I will not blame my loving parents or supportive family for any of my own mistakes. My Bahamian Father and American Mother were young, crazy in love teenagers when they began their journey into parenthood around 16 years old. My unwed mother dropped out of high school in the 10th grade. My Father worked from sunup to sundown. His most notable job was for Waste Management as a garbageman. Our home was full of laughter, love, and arguments. The arguments were about money and how we did not have enough of it. I remember our first apartment was a two-bedroom dream! We had bunk beds and a huge closet! At times life in my mind was perfect. Our reality was not perfect, but tolerable. Tolerable because I was raised with both my parents who provided for me to the best of their abilities. Money was always tight as there were three mouths to feed, clothes to buy, and always a pending shut off notice that refused to be ignored. I knew things would not always be this way. My Grandma Emma and Mother always spoke of finding the silver lining in every situation. My mother would say, "Dale, look on the bright side", as a way of encouraging me to find hope in every situation as tears streamed down her own face.

As an adolescent, I spent my teenage years running my life down the drain as I partied at teen clubs, drinking alcohol, and eventually smoking marijuana. I was dropped from the cheerleading team my junior year of high school. Losing my spot as a high school cheerleader sent a crushing blow of reality that I was not prepared for. I was not prepared for any type of transition mentally. I partied in high school due to my lack of self-control and positive stress coping mechanisms. Losing my spot on the cheerleading team crushed my dreams of being a professional Dallas Cowboys cheerleader. My entire self-worth was wrapped in my popularity as a high school cheerleader. I was a "local celebrity". Everyone knew Debraca. Would losing my spot on the team cause me to be forgotten?

I barely graduated from high school with a 2.04 GPA. I smiled along with my classmates not realizing the world was bigger than Boynton Beach, Florida. After graduation, my biggest emotional abyss happened, I broke up with my high school sweetheart Peanut. I felt lost and unsure of where my life was headed. I wallowed around for a year, before my sister Darvina asked my Mom to send me to Tallahassee for a summer getaway. Of course, my older sister knew I needed a break from the everyday drama that was Debraca inspired. I went to Tallahassee and never looked back. The change in scenery did not do much to change my focus, my outlook on life, or my desire to become more than "Dat Baby".

In 2003, I gave birth to my son Darvin Harris. After my son's delivery, I looked over at my Mother singing to this little guy that would change my life forever. She told my son she loved him and that she

 would always be there until her dying day. I saw how selfless my mother was, raising us. I knew I had a lot to learn and fast. I realized I had to make my mark in life, so I decided to finish what I started and get my education.

In 2004, I went back to school as a freshman at Tallahassee Community College. I was determined to finish what I had started years prior. After graduation from Tallahassee Community College, I applied for admission to Florida State University as a Consumer Science Textile student in other words, a Fashion Major. As I completed the online application, I kept questioning myself saying, "Debraca why are you doing this"? "You are never getting into Florida State University". "You are not smart enough to get in". Randomly checking my email, I realized my acceptance letter arrived that Friday and my classes started on Monday. I could not believe I was going to be a student at Florida State University in the Fashion Merchandising tract.

My life was perfectly imperfect. I was trying to raise my son using the village mentality. I depended heavily on my network of friends to get things organized for my son. I used my financial aid as the foundation to keep the lights on, pay rent, and keep food in our stomachs. When I walked into those doors at Florida State University; I walked in knowing I could not leave without that degree! My Mom always taught me, go hard, or go home. You throw everything you have at it until you accomplish what you set out to finish. In my head, I was 26 years old sitting in a classroom full of happy people who I thought had perfect lives.

What my classmates did not know was I worked a full-time job at Comcast Cable and a part time job at Ross Dress for Less while tolerating the mental torment of my son's Father. I did not fall asleep in class because I was lazy or partying all night. Waking up early to take my son to the bus stop at 5am after working until 11pm the night before was my reason for falling asleep during class. My brother/cousin Patrick would help keep Darvin a few nights a week and drop him off at the bus stop in the morning. Patrick always looked for ways to make things easier for me. He taught Darvin things I could not. He taught Darvin how to handle his temperament and how to manage his feelings of anger or disappointment as a black male child. Patrick also taught Darvin how to use his words to express his feelings and not bottle them up to throw them away. Patrick lived by the motto: a closed mouth, don't get fed. As you can imagine the lessons of Uncle Patrick were foundational. Patrick was my go-to person in the village for support.

The second in command of the village was Janada. Janada was my best friend and Darvin's God Mom. Janada made sure her footprints of beliefs and ideas that would be imprinted on my son. She never missed a moment to help. She made my son love reading because they read books consistently. His imagination is amazing because they created elaborate stories and took turns completing the endings. Janada gave with her heart. She gave Darvin a foundation she envisioned would make him successful in life. As this giving woman never turned her back on Darvin she also never judged me for any of my failures in parenting. She found a way of encouraging me to fix my mistakes with positive suggestions that led to productive outcomes. In no way am I complaining about my motherhood journey, path, or struggles; My emotional struggles in co-parenting strengthened the mental muscles and resilience I would later need in Corporate America.

I was not the typical FSU student. I did not want to be labeled the single black Mom. I wanted to be the student who learned wisdom from all her mistakes. I discovered I was more than a party girl. I was a woman with value. Ultimately, the label I did not want attached as my social ruler was my best tool. I used the title of single mother, full time employee, and full-time college graduate to land several offers after graduation in 2009.

I used my single Mom life as the foundation in my interviews to highlight how I was resilient and tenacious when others would not be. I was seasoned at life. I highlighted my life as a journey other student could have not traveled due to their age and social status. I reminded interviewers my resilience with unplanned situations is what made me as durable as classrooms' carpet – extremely tough! I highlighted how my upbeat personality and tenacity for life would keep me excited about

hiring, training, and coaching Rockstar employees.

In no way was I ready to transition from high school, to college, to parenthood, or anything else. There was no guide that said, if you want to do this, do that. No one prepared me for what was next after high school. I had idea of what I wanted or thought I wanted. I did not have a road map to follow or even think of following. I rolled, fell, struggled, and stammered until it all came together.

I am a single unwed mother of an amazing 17-year-old son. I hold three degrees. I am an entrepreneur and Certified Career Coach. I am blessed to experience teaching moments along my journey learning to endure through the pain is what made me the woman I am today.

Writing this book is my sincere investment in you, in your child, and in their future! I want to share tips and secrets with you, that will help you navigate the path with your teen to their next step in life.

Guiding you from one stage to another is one of life's biggest challenges. What path is right for your student and why? What if your child chooses trade school or the military? Did you fail as a parent?

Solid facts and guidance are what this book will supply you and your student. The only request is you realize there is no perfect situation. Life happens, so know that your love and support is what will propel life forward for your teen regardless of the path they chose.

DEDICATION
THE LESSON A SON TEACHES HIS MOM
DEBRACA RUSSELL MBA CPCC

Thank You Omari, Mr. Harris, Darvin, D, Momma's Man, Sunshine, and Chipmunk. Okay, okay, I guess I should not tell all the names I have for you on such a public forum, but you know how much I love you for just being... YOU!

I sincerely thank those villagers that have kept my son, Darvin, so I could study, sleep, or simply be Debraca. Being a college graduate is a title I own because I had others that believed in me enough to invest in me. I thank the villagers that purchased groceries when I did not have the means. I thank the villagers that lent money for gas when my tank was as empty as my heart from life's heartbreaks. I thank the villagers that listened to me cry, whine, and complain when I was being shaken and molded for more.

No words can ever repay the time, love, and energy you invested in me or my visions. I know my life is not my own, my life will continue to serve as a stark example about choices, and reactions. I made my choices to endure the reactions to my actions. Darvin has always been my best choice and will always be my most valuable action!

ACKNOWLEDGMENTS

Acknowledging three coauthors that invested their time while supporting my vision to provide a book that would give answers and solutions to parents, adoptive parents, grandparent, aunts, uncles, or foster parents on how they can help their student succeed. Zaneta Ellison LMHC, I thank you for using your expertise to educate the readers of this book about mental health, healthy transition, and coping mechanisms for their student. Your endless nights of writing to rewrite your chapter echoed your passion for your craft and educating others. Allison Haviland, thank you for opening your heart and journey in life highlighting your untraditional path through the educational system. I know your motherly tone will warm the hearts of our readers while educating them on best practices surrounding financial aid and student loans. Javed Morgan, I thank you for financial education. Educating our readers about responsible spending, prevention of debt and ways to save will lead to their prosperous futures.

No amount of thanks spoken or written can equal the amount of appreciation for Leslie Reed. She answered my call, well text, for assistance to ensure this book would be a solid resource that our educational institutions, parents, and guardians would support. Leslie gave me a non-filtered reality check. Leslie, I thank you for being a voice of reason and one of my cheerleaders. You are appreciated madam!

RESOURCES

New Vision Behavioral Health Inc. is a private behavioral health agency, created to provide mental health treatment, crisis interventions, and overall holistic wellness. We provide individualized, evidence-based treatment, and care to our clients. Our Mission is to improve the lives of people with behavioral health needs through the efficient and effective provision of quality services delivered with respect, dignity, cultural sensitivity, and a focus on recovery. Owner and operator Zaneta Ellison LMHC is a licensed Mental Health Counselor who has several years of experience working with children, at-risk youth, and adults with mental health and addiction disorders, in addition to the offender-ex-offender population. Zaneta coins herself as a Transitional therapist and relationship trauma coach. Her work as a Therapist and coach is to support, uplift, encourage and bring healing to the lives of others; to assist individuals to move past their deepest, and intimate place of pain, and thrive in all relationships. Her work enables others to see past their present circumstances and strive towards healing with intention, authenticity, clarity, and over all mental-emotional wellness.

Zaneta Ellison LMHC CEO
New Vision Behavioral Health Inc.

WE ARE HERE TO HELP!

Our Services

Transitional Counseling & Trauma Informed Care

Offender/Ex-offender Services
FDOC Vendor

Youth & School Based Services

Contact Our Clinic Directly ☎ 727-687-0997

Why Choose Us?

At New Vision Behavioral Health Inc., we can help you discover a better life by helping you cope with or even resolve your current life circumstances and re-create your life visions of success and wellness.

Our individualized services, and competent staff, will assist with an ongoing improvement of health and wellness.

Private Pay Options

● Cigna, Humana, Medicaid, Aetna, Optum, Various EAP's.

● New Vision Behavioral Health Inc. provides you with the highest quality, cost-effective medical care

● At New Vision Behavioral Health Inc, we are Fostering a Vision for Change.

• Individual > Group > Family > Couples Counseling

www.newvisionbehavioralhealth.org   info@newvisionbehavioralhealth.com xgmail.com

Zaneta Ellison LMHC, CEO New Vision Behavioral Health Inc.
727-687-0997
www.newvisionbehavioralhealth.com

At Wealthwave it is our mission to stamp out financial illiteracy so people can make confident decisions with their money, create a work-optional lifestyle, and have a better shot at living the American Dream. We teach people how to put money to work for themselves instead of just working for money. We educate and provide products with solutions ranging from Life Insurance, Investing, Estate Planning, College Planning and Retirement Planning.

Javed Morgan, Financial Advisor Wealthwave
Wealthwave.com/javedmorgan

Contents

Chapter 6 - Javed Morgan

Chapter 7 - Debraca Russell MBA CPCC

Resources

Introduction
- Debraca Russell MBA CPCC

CHOOSING MY LEGACY

Standing in the hallway of his grandparent's house listening as they say the most hurtful phrase you can say to a child, "It's ok, everyone is not college material". Steven hears these words as the final step in his downward spiral to the (I don't care) IDC zone. Everyone is not college material is a fable we use to express disappointment in our son or daughter. I heard this statement myself almost 23 years ago from my high school counselor when my final grades were posted. She did not feel I could do anything. "Was she right?" All I felt was anger, hurt, and shame. I wanted to start cursing to protect my crushed dreams of being a college cheerleader. Cheerleading was my life outside of running track. To be "nice", I kept my frustrations to myself and walked away. Muddling my hurt and disappointment, this was my only coping mechanism.

I walked home with my best friend Keisa. She told me that I could do whatever I wanted. Keisa said, "Deb you're awesome don't listen to her"! For the remainder of the afternoon, we talked about why I needed to be more responsible and stop blaming others for my shortfalls. I was a proficient victim. I was the youngest of three children and I knew how to "play hurt" whenever needed. My parents are separating, I am stressed, and I can't... that was my go-to excuse for EVERYTHING I did not want to partake in. If I got a C, Keisa's response was, "Really Deb REALLY"? Keisa made me feel like I was only hurting myself and she was not going to stand by and watch the downfall. Secretly I "wished" I was focused like Keisa. She made the impossible seem easy like Sunday morning.

As I previously mentioned, I graduated with a 2.04 GPA. Was I proud of myself? Was I going to walk across that stage with my head held high? Was I going to smile as I walked in my cap and gown? Short answer, YEP! I earned something no one thought I would. I had tons of naysayers that were laying the foundation for my demise, well that was what I thought. If people did not sing my praise; I automatically assumed they were my enemy. My coping mechanism for failing at anything was to blame the "haters" instead of saying I let myself down. I needed to adjust my concept of support and understand support happens whenever, wherever, and from whoever. I had to make a choice but did not know how. What should I do after graduation? The school counselors were busy helping "real graduates" so I got the courtesy that these are your options conversation. Which was followed up with the let us know if you need anything else.

What happens if I went to the military? Can I attend trade school? Do I have to leave home and get my own place to be considered an adult? I was prepared to debate everyone that opposed my decision. Whoever uttered these horrible words with the idea that college is a prize and that anyone that chooses another path was doomed to a long life of poverty. If you believe you are not college material; what type of material are you? Are you polyester? Are you cotton? You are not an article of clothing; therefore, the phrase college material does not exist as a prediction to your value or self-worth.

I suggest open ended questions such as: Do you like your classes? Do you enjoy completing your classwork or homework? Of course, interrogating your teen is not your motivation, but finding out what they enjoy about education is. If they answered no or not at all you may want to consider other avenues outside the traditional educational setting for your teen.

Millions of people believe in manifestation, speaking life into a situation or that their path is ordained by God. Planning is mandatory to make an effective decision. As a high school student, your teen is bombarded with social media videos, online blogs, and gorilla marketing telling them what is best, popular, or the next best thing that's lit.

Getting to know your adolescent is the most powerful tool you can use when you communicate your desires, dreams, and fears to them. Everyone wants to be heard and understood. Understanding your teen will make communicating more effective as they will feel like you are not barking commands or demands at them; you are discussing their future with them. Asking the tough questions and listening is the hardest job imaginable. It is so easy to say what they will do and how they will do it with the idea that you are helping them "make the best decision".

I am currently having this conversation with my son, to find out what he wants his life to "look like" after high school? How much money do you want to make per year? Do you have a desired goal for owning a home or building one from the ground up? Do you want to be a Father? Do you want to work for yourself or someone else? I asked a myriad of questions making Darvin feel like I was interrogating him. Asking questions back-to-back could make your teen feel like you are "coming down" on them. Basic fight or flight response will kick in and things could go awry.

I tried various other approaches to steal the secrets of Darvin's desires with no success. My initial approach resulted in an epic failure. My idea of helping Darvin discover what he wanted was met with his own line of questioning better known as defense. Number 42 defensive tackle from the Junior Buccaneers suited back up in his shoulder pads, cleats, and helmet to protect his thoughts pertaining to his future career. "Mom, why are you asking me all these questions"? Which led to his final statement, "You make it seem like I am graduating tomorrow". Insert mic drop, Darvin let me know he knew and would share in his own time.

Darvin asked, "What if I don't want to go to college"? "Would you be mad"? "Can I not go and figure something out later"? After catching my breath from dodging his barrage of questioning, I realized I needed to find another approach. I spoke with several teachers and other parents to see how I could ask my son questions and get realistic answers. When speaking with my best friend Christine, she spoke about how she navigated this conversation with her son. He did not see the value in following his mother's footsteps to obtain a bachelor's degree. He went to Lincoln Tech Technical school in Nashville, Tennessee and received his certification in Heavy Machinery. By pursuing his education at an accredited technical school, he found his passion, and has a successful career making good money all while avoiding the most common obstacle of college, **"THE DEBT"**.

I consulted an adolescent therapist, who suggested my tone with Darvin be light, fluid, and non-threatening in nature. He was spot on! Darvin opened his "little black book" of ideas and told me how and what he wanted. The questions I asked Darvin led him to his own soul searching and self-evaluation. Make the conversation as non-scripted as possible.

If you need help finding a therapist in your area you could ask your teen's school counselor. If the counselor does not offer any referrals, you can ask your student's pediatrician. If your teens doctor does not offer a suitable referral you can search Psychology Today *(https://www.psychologytoday.com/us/therapists/child-or-adolescent)*. The website will allow you to search for a licensed therapist in your area. Another great idea would be to ask other caregivers if they have any suggestions for a therapist as well.

Parents, please keep in mind all teens are not the same. I am sure you have heard the old verbiage, "There is no rule book to parenting". You can open the doors of communication or close them. Keep these lines open to get the best responses regardless of the outcome of this initial Question & Answer session. Parents we need to start the conversation sooner rather than later as time becomes a factor when your teen is in their junior or senior year.

Career planning does not have to be difficult. I repeat, career planning does not have to be difficult. Career planning can be as simple as using Google to search for potential jobs such as a Plumber, Electrician, CNC machinist, Network specialist, Elevator repair, Installation specialist, Transportation manager, Logistics manager, Office assistant, or Welder if you don't think you want to attend college. If you think college is not an option for your student, search for occupations in the Occupational handbook *(https://www.bls.gov/ooh/)* or O*Net Online *(https://www.onetonline.org)*. These two sources offer an endless array of information like projected employment demand or decreases along with the average salary ranges.

Your students' high school education is important because it sets the foundation for their future. Traditional high school versus homeschooling has been the debate for more than 30 years. Do homeschool students excel more than traditionally educated students? The next section we speak about some facts about home school and next steps for your teen.

Chapter 1 - Debraca Russell MBA CPCC

HOMESCHOOL LIFE: ATTENDING HIGH SCHOOL FROM MY ROOM

Statistics show homeschooling students are a growing population that cannot and will not be ignored in the world of academia. According to the Business Insider article, Charter schools have become a significant part of the US public-education system and now educate 2.5 million kids.

Data from the National Center for Education Statistics and analysis from Brian Ray, a homeschooling researcher at the National Home Education Research Institute, suggest the number of kids taught at home is growing by 3% to 8% a year since the total hovered around 1.8 million in 2012, according to data from the National Center for Education Statistics. That puts the upper estimate at approximately 3.5 million children, far surpassing charter schools.

Homeschooling is not a perfect walk in the park. Homeschooling your student does come with a new collection of obstacles to navigate. In the past accredited colleges and universities were hesitant to enroll homeschooled students as their curriculum is "different and unpredictable". One could imagine that colleges assumed homeschooled students would not know enough of the foundational content of history, science, and other common core subjects.

The homeschool World History class may or may not have the same content, therefore your student may be taxed with learning content in college that they should have learned in high school. Is this a big enough hurdle to prevent a school from accepting your student's GPA or transcripts for enrollment? Will your student need to prove they have earned and completed the necessary requirements for high school graduation based upon what they were taught? The answer to these questions is yes!

Historically homeschool students struggled when competing for college scholarships. The integrity of the GPA is based on trust. Does the scholarship board believe your student earned that 4.0 GPA as they were taught outside the public or private school system? There are several laws that regulate homeschooling your student. This creates a level playing field. Homeschooled students must abide by the same record keeping practices as the traditional school.

"It's really important that a home-schooled student shares with us a really detailed account as to how they came to be a home-schooled student and what they've done with their time as one," says Brittney Dorow, assistant dean of admission at Colgate University. "And that's going to come in a transcript that they have written out, which will detail a trajectory as well as the classes that they've taken and give an explanation of what those courses are."

{Article, https://www.usnews.com/education/best-colleges/articles/
2018-07-18/how-home-schooling-affects-college-admissions}.

The suggestion to homeschooling parents is to document, document, and document some more. Make sure you can show how your student performed and why they would be a great candidate for higher education options. The details of your curriculum should be highlighted to show how your student excelled in a nontraditional environment which lends to their creativity. Home school students have the same options after high school as a traditional high school student such as the military, college, vocational school, or trade school.

Prior to graduation you will want to consider if your teen will take the ACT or SAT as a part of their college submission package. Most schools offer financial waivers to absorb the cost for families that receive free or reduced lunch benefits. In some school districts your teen can take these standardized tests during their school day. Visit the school district website for your county to see if this is an option for your student. As things are changing to include more options for graduating seniors there are currently 27 colleges and universities do not require standardized test scores for admission.

Colorado College	George Mason University
Smith College	Wesleyan University
Marist College	Wake Forest University
Bowdoin College	New York University
Ithaca College	St. John's University
American University	Texas Tech University
University of Delaware	Connecticut College
Rollins College	James Madison University
Brandeis University	Loyola University Maryland
University of Puget Sound	University of Arizona
College of the Holy Cross	University of Texas Austin
University of Evansville	George Washington University
University of South Dakota	University of Chicago
California State University	

Some colleges believe students should not get accepted or denied college acceptance with standardized test scores alone. A few colleges on the list have waived this requirement. The colleges that waived the test scored requirement require your teen to write an essay indicating why they should be accepted. Another way your teen can omit the standardized test is by being in the top 10% of their graduating class.

DUAL ENROLLMENT:
THE FREE ASSOCIATES DEGREE

Dual enrollment also called concurrent enrollment, are programs that allow students to be enrolled in two separate, academically related institutions. Generally, it refers to high school students taking college or university courses. If your student has the required GPA requirements, dual enrollment at the local community college could be a great tool to utilize, I highly encourage it! The chance to get any college credits out of the way while still in high school at no cost, its priceless. I personally have echoed the regret of wanting to do things differently while still in high school- Allison Haviland. It will give your teen a jump start in their career journey. The dual enrollment process can start their freshman year if you feel your teen is strong enough to handle the demands of the program. You simply contact your student's guidance counselor for the paperwork. Once the paperwork is completed and submitted, your student must take a test to gauge what classes they would be qualified or eligible to take. Once the classes are determined your student is free to register with the school approval each semester at the Community College or University of their choice.

Suggested college courses are dependent on how your student scores on their entrance exam. If your student scores well they would be able to take English I and II (ENC 1101/ ENC 1102), College Success, along with other introduction courses. I suggest talking with your student about the demands and importance of staying committed to both schools to ensure success. Your student will need to create a schedule or calendar of study times and dates for their subjects. Remind your teen to communicate with their college professor to ensure they are not lost in the shuffle of students on campus. College professors will expect the same level of work from your high school student that they expect from the other students. Your teen will grow mentally and emotionally by dual enrolling as their high school environment is different from their college environment. Your student will develop a sense of independence, accountability, and self-awareness from this new step.

References

- *www.fastweb.com*
- *www.raise.me*
- *www.unigo.com*

1. The National Association of Student Financial Aid Administrators: *http://www.nasfaa.org/*. This site provides comprehensive

information about financial aid for students, including programs from each state.

2. The National Center for Education Statistics: *http://nces.ed.gov/*. This site provides information on tuition, room and board, and other fees for every college and university in the United States.

3. The College Affordability and Transparency Center: *http://collegecost.ed.gov/*. A terrific site that helps students determine the cost of colleges and universities, make comparisons between different institutions, and help figure out which schools are affordable for them.

4. United States Department of Education: *http://www.ed.gov/college-completion*

In the next chapter we examine how college is not the choice for every student. Trade schools or vocational schools are equally good decisions for your student without the large price tag. Remember your student does not have to fit into any "perfect mold". Your son or daughter needs to stay true to their passion for their career transition and whatever it looks like for them.

Parents, Guardians, and Caretakers as you read through these chapters, give yourself permission to feel the stress of uncertainty and the excitement of change. You are not omitted. If you want to sing, cry, or scream; do it knowing this is a positive way to express emotion. Life is transiting, stress, and anxiety may be present at the table. The next chapter will highlight how stress can affect your student in this period of life's transition. Most people would tell you this generation of teens is weak and needs to get "toughened up". I caution you not to think this way. When you are hurting, being hurt, or scared, do you relish in the pain or do you try to find solutions to end it? This generation of adolescents is dealing with and tolerating stressors differently than you may have in your adolescence. Today social media, peer pressure, and the "acceptance of bullying" has made things quite interesting.

Our country, our society, and our generation are collectively hurting. The evidence of our hurt is evident in our actions, reactions, and our individually self-absorbed decisions.

Parents continue with an open mind as you read the next chapter.

Licensed Mental Health Counselor Zaneta N. Ellison has her own practice in Florida, where she helps adults understand and assist with their teen's transitions. Zaneta excels in her career as she has personally used her advice with her own children. Zaneta will explain and discuss tips to help your teen with coping mechanisms.

Chapter 2 - Zaneta Ellison, LMHC

SUPPORTING THE MENTAL AND EMOTIONAL SHIFTS

You have done it! Your student is ready! It is time for the child you birthed, raised, fostered, or adopted to leave the nest. You wake them up for school, got them out the door, and even helped with completing homework during their roller coaster ride of pubescent emotions. Congratulations your job is still not done, but you have been promoted from caregiver to encourager or confidant!

You have inflicted consequences, taken away privileges, and had to ban friends. Mom, Dad, Grandmother, Uncle, Aunt, Guardian, or Foster parent whoever you are, you have done everything you could to get your teen prepared for their coming days. Your teen is not only walking across the stage of graduation, but they are about to cross over the stage of life towards independence, and adulthood. Now I know for some of you, this transition can be scary for both you and your teen for many reasons. Regardless of the feelings associated with this transition, you realize that the transition must occur.

As adults, most of us understand by now that before new things can begin, old things must end. We cannot expect to experience new beginnings unless we are willing to release old experiences. As we mature through this life, from birth to death, we will experience a variety of phases and stages of life. Phases of life that are necessary, vital, and interconnected one to another. As your student plans for that great escape from your supervision, many of them have somehow created this image of what they think freedom will be like. As appealing as the opportunity is to be free from the reigns of parents and guardians, as well experienced adults; your student may not be truly ready right after graduation. These expected shifts in responsibilities can unexpectedly become overwhelming to any transitioning young adult. While watching your young adult transition into an independent adulthood; it certainly requires that we carefully assist our graduate with navigating the mental-emotional shift accompanied this transition. This chapter will discuss the realistic statistics that graduates face when it comes to various post graduate transitions. We will explore effective mental-emotional and cognitive strategies that would assist you and your graduate with navigating the transition from high school into independent living successfully. Lastly, we will explore change from a Transitional Model perspective. You will also read about how Emotional Intelligence could help your student navigate the transition from high school mentally and emotionally intact.

I always tell my college age clients that adjusting to the changes of their new life experiences requires a willingness to effectively engage in their process of transitioning.

I can honestly admit that it was not until my graduate school studies that I realized that I was not good at adjusting to change and was completely resistant to transitioning. I absolutely dreaded and did my best to avoid experiencing change as much as humanly possible. Based on my childhood traumas of divorce, abuse, and abandonment, I developed a toxic way of doing things to manipulate, control others, and outcomes to my detriment. As a result of this foolish behavior, I ruined relationships, sabotaged opportunities, exhausted myself mentally, and emotionally. In my mind change equated to turmoil and pain, and it left me feeling anxious, fearful, sad, lingering in places, and with people I was long overdue to let go of.

Let us explore some facts. According to the U.S. Bureau of Labor Statistics, 69.1 percent of 2018 high school graduates aged 16 to 24 were enrolled in colleges or universities. According to College Atlas,

70 percent of Americans will study at a four-year college, but less than two-thirds will graduate with a degree. Thirty percent of college freshmen drop out after their first year of school, while 57% of students enrolled in college are not done after six years. Of that 57%, 33% of them drop out entirely; leaving the remaining 24% enrolled as either full time or part time students. In short, starting college does not guarantee your teen will continue until they graduate in four years or even six years. Offering your teen support is necessary to help them succeed with their intended goal. As stated earlier, encouraging your students to be open with their communication and emotions will assist with helping them feel supported. Support their decision to pursue an education at a two-year or four-year institution, trade school, vocational school, or the military. Our teens are bombarded with social media and the images that are trending: It is cooler to vape versus smoke cigarettes, mixed drinks are better than the "hard stuff". These phrases are commonly heard in the hallways at school unfortunately. Ongoing discussions about drugs and alcohol with your teen will help them not be on the negative end of the statistical charts.

The National Institute of Drug Abuse completed a survey amongst college age adults ages 19-22. Their studies found that marijuana use amongst this population was at historic highs. In 2018, 42.6% for college age students and 42.5% non-college age students used marijuana. Approximately one in nine non-college adults reported daily or near daily use, (11.1%) compared to about one in 17 college students (5.9%). In 2018, 28% of college students and 25% of non-college adults reported binge drinking. Binge drinking is consuming large amounts of alcohol or liquor in a short period of time. Outside of social drug use and alcohol is nicotine vaping. Between 2017 and 2018, nicotine vaping increased in college students from 6.1% to 15.5% and from 7.9% to 12.5% in non-college adults. The dangerous link of substance abuse can be amplified with the presence of mental disorders. Anxiety, depression, and stress were the primary concerns of students who visited college counseling centers during the 2017-2018, and the same for the 2018-2019 academic year as reported by clinicians working in counseling centers. In the 2017-2018 academic term, 50% of students who stopped attending college did so due to mental health-related reasons.

Unfortunately, the previously mentioned data is related to adolescent peer pressure. Encouraging your teen to remain firm in their decision to not use drugs and alcohol is key to supporting their sprint to success. The statistics can be reduced by giving your teen an outlet to release the stress and tools to use. Counseling or therapy can help your teen explore or discover triggers that could lead to drug use. Reducing stress is another way to help your teen. Stress can be reduced with exercise, laughter, and healthy eating. Identifying new support systems, meaningful connections with people that understand the dangers of drugs and alcohol can encourage them to remain firm.

Our newly enlisted military cadets also experience the same feelings of separation and isolation in their transition as well. The emotion is the same. Numerous military support programs offer confidential counseling to service members and their families. A counselor can also teach you how to cope with stress and grief. Military One-Source, Tricare, and Real Warriors can be helpful resources for your military teen.

The terms Change and Transitions in the Cambridge Dictionary are defined as Change is to make or become different or get one thing in place of another thing." Oxford defines Transition as a change from one form or type to another, or the process by which this happens. Therefore, transitioning is the internal process involved in one's place of change.

THE TRANSITION MODEL

A business consultant by the name of William Bridges created a Transition Model by the name of the *Bridges Transition Model*. Bridges focused on the difference between change and transitioning. He concluded that change was something that happened to everyone. He stated that change is inevitable and comes whether you agree with it or not. However, transition on the other hand was the internal shift that happens in people's minds as they go through changes and can occur a lot slower than change itself. Bridges derived that change occurred in three stages, which he named Phrase One, Two, and Three.

Phase One- **Ending, Losing, and Letting go** (moving out of the home, relocating to another city, state, or country). In phase One, we are realizing, accepting, and understanding that something is coming or has come to an end, and realizing that it is time to let go. For example, as a Senior in high school, in Bridges phase one of change, would seek closure in leaving behind their high school years and their time as a teen under the rulership of their caregivers. This would include the ending of the time they would spend with childhood friends and family. In this phase they would be disengaging in activities and routines that they had become accustomed to as youth and once found fulfillment in. In this phase, most people would experience a various number of feelings and emotions that ranged from sadness, confusion, doubt, and fear. In this phase, the weight of trying to let go these experiences often become a bit overwhelming to manage and grasp.

Phase Two -**The Neutral Zone**. This is the bridge between what we left (family/home, geographical location, friends, relationships) and what we are walking into (college, career, military, independent living, making new relationships). It is the gap between the old and the new life experiences. Here a person may experience resentment towards change or others whom they feel are "forcing" their change. They may experience low productivity or motivation, anxiety about their new identity, and role in life, in addition to skepticism towards change. This phase is considered the "core" of the transition process. This is the time that they are identifying how they will create new ways of living, learning, growing, relating, and connecting. They are figuring out what it means to live independently and outside of your ruling, leadership, and care.

Phase Three -The last phase to Bridges Model of Transition is **New Beginnings**. Yes, it is as beautiful as it sounds. In New Beginnings, your young adult, will have developed into their new role and identity. They would have flourished from the end of one phase of life into the start of another. They are walking into that light at the end of the tunnel so to speak. In this phase they embrace new behaviors, new ways of living, and being. They learn how to function as a full-time adult student, an active member of the military, or just navigate through career and work demands. They learn to become their own steward!

So, I know some of you may be saying, "Zaneta, what would that look like for me and my teen? How do I effectively assist my graduate with transitioning out of the home and thriving through their next life venture?" I am so glad you asked. Let us explore some helpful tips and tools that will help your student navigate their life transition, while maintaining mental and emotional wellness.

STEPS TO SUCCESSFULLY NAVIGATE TRANSITIONS THROUGH EMOTIONAL INTELLIGENCE

Evidence supports that emotional intelligence can create stronger relationships, win at school, work, and achieve your career, and personal goals. Emotional intelligence is the catalyst to help you to connect with your feelings, be action focused, and make informed decisions about what matters most to you. The art of becoming emotionally intelligent involves building Self-Awareness, Social Awareness, Self-Management, and Relationship Management. It is the ability to understand, manage, and utilize your own emotions in positive ways to relieve stress, effectively communicate and empathize with others, overcome challenges, and manage conflict. This ability is vital to a successful transition and navigation to your next stage of life after high school. Let's review the 5 steps that I identified as key steps to transitioning.

Step 1: **Practice Acceptance**: *When your graduate is in the season of ending and letting go.*

You nor your graduate can afford to ignore the change that is about to occur. When we refuse to accept change (rather planned, predicted, or caught off guard), we become STUCK and unproductive.

Your graduate must accept the reality that life as they know it is changing and they must prepare their minds first for that change. This involves an open and outward acknowledgement that a change needs or must occur and allow themselves to connect with the feelings, and emotions attached to that realization. If it's fear you feel, feel it! If it's sadness, confusion, or disappointment, acknowledge it! Whatever the feeling maybe, don't deny it, don't fight it, and don't judge it. Be genuine about the impact this change is having in your life and connect with someone who can support you during this time.

Step 2: **Assess the Situation**: It is vital that your graduate identify the behaviors, routines, lifestyle choices that will need to change, and identify those things that can continue existing as they embark on their new journey. Clearly mark and define your endings.

Step 3: **Align your thinking**: Whether you are in the beginning phase of change, or in the neutral zone, there is a mental shift that must occur. To accept the ending and embrace the new beginning, they must prepare and develop a mindset that embraces that shift. Do you need to adjust your thinking to be more independent? Do you need to prepare your mind to accept and deal with authority and restricted freedom (this would be necessary if you are joining the military or falling under some other form of authority or leadership)? Do you need to shift to a mindset that is confident and willing to take risks (this mindset is especially beneficial if you are pursuing entrepreneurship)?

Whatever type of change you are experiencing, you will have to create a mindset that aligns, prepares, and supports your transitioning.

Step 4: **Identify Goals and Milestones**: In the process of change and transition, it is most helpful if you spend time reflecting and focusing on creating a plan. What do you want to work towards accomplishing? What are your targets and tangible goals? What would you like to see occur out of this transition from one place in life to the next? What would it look like once you have successfully crossed the bridge of where you are to where you would like to be? Visualizing your future and identifying a plan to work towards achieving your goals allows you to strategically make the necessary changes for growth and maturity.

Step 5: **Manage your time with Intention**: During the season of transitioning, it is important that you plan and prioritize your time. To not become roped into doing too much and becoming overwhelmed and doing too little. Becoming stagnant is easy. It is important to focus on what is important to you in this season and remain focused on those things. Avoid the unnecessary distractions in life of people, things, habits that will trip you up, get you off course, and away from your mission.

Step 6: **Release and clear any limiting beliefs and people**: It is our belief systems that shape our feelings and our behaviors. If you want to experience positivity, you must be willing to release negative beliefs, ideals, and relationships that bring you negativity. Self-doubt, self-defeat, limited thinking, expecting the worst, catastrophizing, making things bigger or worse than they need to be are nothing shy of self-destructive. Negative and toxic relationships are also traps that will keep you stuck in limbo and distracted from change and growth. Negative belief systems will make transitioning a draining, dreadful, and complicated experience.

In conclusion, as part of maturating and developing through life, there is an acknowledgment and acceptance that one season must end for the other to begin. In this acceptance, we embrace the realities of change and actively participate in the mental-emotional process of that change. As caregivers and parents, it is our responsibility to help our students successfully navigate this shift with wisdom, integrity, and an openness to failure, to learn, and to grow into independent men and women. Although it can be difficult for us to watch our young adults struggle during any part of their life, we rest easier when we know that we have created a healthy foundation and equipped them with tools and awareness of how to appropriately manage and thrive through their transitional process.

VISUALIZATION EXERCISE

Engage in an exercise that allows you to visualize your place of change and transition. What would that place look like for you? What do they feel when they are in that place? What do you feel when you think about the season you are leaving? What emotions come to mind as you visualize that relationship ending, that situation changing, that relocation, leaving friends and family? Allow yourself to sit with those thoughts and feelings. Don't reject them, don't judge them, don't beat yourself up about them, just picture them in your mind.

Now visualize your "New Beginnings". Picture your ideal place of living. Imagine what that place would look like? Where would you be and what would you be doing? What obstacles or hurdles did you have to go through to get to that point? What strengths did you have to tap into to get to that goal?   What did you have to lose or let go of to get there? Just sit in that space for a couple of minutes. Feel the energy from those thoughts and receive you in that space. You've earned that space; you've worked hard to be there. This place in your life was proposed just for you. Now take a deep breath, open your eyes, and prepare yourself for the work ahead of you.

REFERENCE PAGE

Source: National Institute on Drug Abuse; National Institutes of Health; U.S. Department of Health and Human Services. *https://www.drugabuse.gov/related-topics/trends-statistics/infographics/drug-alcohol-use-in-college-age-adults-in-2018*

https://www.activeminds.org/about-mental-health/statistics/

https://www.innovativeeducators.org/blogs/news/just-the-facts-10-concerning-mental-health-stats-about-college-students

Center for Collegiate Mental Health, January 2019. 2018 Annual Report (Publication No. STA 19-180). *https://sites.psu.edu/ccmh/files/2019/01/2018-Annual-Report-1.30.19-ziytkb.pdf*

https://ccmh.psu.edu/files/2020/01/2019-CCMH-Annual-Report.pdf

Improving Emotional Intelligence (EQ) *https://www.helpguide.org/articles/mental-health/emotional-intelligence-eq.htm*

https://www.healthline.com/health/10-ways-to-relieve-stress

Healthline Online Article *https://www.healthline.com/health/depression/military-service#Studies-on-depression-and-violence*

Transitioning is a continuous process as you can see from reading this book. Moving from one aspect of life into another is inevitable because we are alive. With growth comes a cost. A cost of time, money, or dedication.

In Chapter three you will learn about viable options that can fund your teen's education.

Chapter 3 - Allison Haviland

SHOW ME THE MONEY

Who is Allison Haviland? What qualifies her to speak about finding money for your teen's education? Does she understand the roller coaster of questions you have and how to resolve them? Keep reading, I assure you, YOU will NOT be disappointed!

Allison Haviland gained multiple FEMA certifications and took on courses in Emergency Management as a freshman in high school. Her college career was framed by September 11th and Hurricane Katrina, instilling a great sense of need to help others. As a college freshman, Allison volunteered as part of the cleanup crew post Katrina in Biloxi, Mississippi. These tragedies helped Allison realize who she was and how powerful she could be as she took college by the horns! Graduating with a Bachelor of Science in Interdisciplinary Sciences with a focus in Sociology with dual minors in Communication and Children and Families.

As a non-traditional student, Allison utilized the resources from the colleges she attended, learning to navigate the different admissions departments, financial aid processes, and program advisors. While Allison started on her higher education journey the fall following her high school graduation, she struggled with balancing her needs as college student. Working full time with several health conditions resulted in her unscheduled breaks from college. Eventually changing schools, relocating to other cities, and navigating different classroom settings Allison discovered she was extremely resilient. Allison did not see these as setbacks rather, successful experiences she could use to build her foundation upon, that would be meaningful.

Attending her final semester at Florida State University as a full time Distance Learning student, she secured a position with Fortis Technical Institute in Jacksonville, Florida. Recently married and starting her family. Allison got promoted from Administrative Assistant to the Executive Director of the Institute, to ultimately become the Student Success Coordinator focusing on the retention and the continued education of students. One main duty of her new position was to complete internal audits of the staff and faculty to ensure federal regulated guidelines were upheld.

Shortly after the birth of her second son, Allison took on an Admissions Coordinator role at CDA Technical Institute helping students finalize their admissions process and coordinate with financial aid to ensure their tuition needs were met. Loving her career in the world of academia, Allison moved on to be the Program Manager/Program Coordinator for Eastern Kentucky University's online version of their Master's in Safety, Security and Emergency Management degree. In this role, Allison was able to shed light on her own experiences as a student and help others find ways to build their degrees into ways that would most benefit them in their career while taking the most direct and cost-effective path possible.

Ready to take on another challenge, Allison has now transitioned her career into human resource in the role of Talent Acquisition Recruiter. This role allows her to work with people trying to leverage their degrees and life experiences, in the workforce. She speaks to clients regularly that wish they had broadened their education in some ways prior to graduation. Her clients' range in fields from blue collar to white collar, and all the greys that lie between. Her background in Higher Education, her own non-traditional path in undergrad gives her a unique perspective to help align employees with employers. Allison's goals are to provide insight on how to make the best decisions based on the options that are available.

FAFSA

FAFSA Free Application for Federal Student Aid is a federal the program your teen could apply for that would give them access to grants and federal funding for two- year and four-year institutions, trade schools, and vocational schools. You can apply online at (*https://studentaid.gov/h/apply-for-aid/fafsa*). The application will ask you questions about your expected financial contribution for your teen. Completing this application will give your teen access to federal grants, in other words, "free money". The application window opens on October 1st and is free to complete. If you are on a website that asks for your credit card information you are not using the correct website. The application will ask you various questions and even require you to upload your federal taxes for the previous year, but will not ask for any form of payment. When asked about your taxes, if you did not file federal taxes and only state taxes you will need to upload that data. The FAFSA must be completed each year to ensure your student gets federal grant funding for their education. Once the form is completed you will receive a confirmation email indicating your student's application is being processed.

STUDENT LOANS:
CAN I BORROW A FEW THOUSAND DOLLARS?

I often quote my former high school science teacher and one of my mentors when I discuss funding an education, "You are your own best investment." Over the years that quote has held a lot of weight for me and the context at which I have taken it has changed. As I continue to work through paying off my own student debt, I wish I had paid a little closer attention to his meaning and really ask what making an investment meant.

Higher education can be is or should I say is expensive? Private, public, traditional, nontraditional, or vocational institutions, all require a financial component so getting any form of formalized education comes at a cost. There are always risks to any investment you make. You are your own best investment and what you put into your career you will get out of it, including your education. The first and most important piece of advice is do not over borrow money for school. If you are in a situation where you need more financial support, utilize student loans for the necessary expenses, but do not borrow money to spend on weekend trips, getaways, partying, or other unnecessary expenses.

It is important to know the difference between the types of loans and what the true cost of these loans are. There are three types of student loans funded by the federal government, Subsidized, Unsubsidized and Perkins loan.

DIRECT SUBSIDIZED LOAN will be the smaller loan amount offered per semester as it is based on perceived financial need from the data entered on your FAFSA. This need is determined by multiple factors such as dependency status, scholarship, grant provisions, and the wealth of the student's parents (tax return will determine this amount). Subsidized student loans do accrue interest (2.75% x the dollar amount of money borrowed = debt grows), but the federal government is paying it while the student is actively enrolled at any educational institution. Once the student is no longer actively enrolled (six-month period) the interest accrues and the student is liable for the total repayment debt.

DIRECT UNSUBSIDIZED LOANS are not considered need based and therefore are offered in larger amounts. They accrue interest day one (after the money is received) and unlike their subsidized counterparts, the student is responsible for the full amount.

PERKINS LOANS (regardless of the first disbursement date) have a fixed interest rate of 5%.

A Perkins loan is a type of federal student loan based on financial need. Perkins loans are available to undergraduate, graduate, and professional students. A Perkins loan is a subsidized loan, meaning that the federal government pays the loan's interest while you are in school. All schools may not participate with this loan option, so please check your educational institution.

Interest rates on federal student loans are set by federal law, not the U.S. Department of Education. In all three cases the loans are deferred during active enrollment, meaning no monthly payments are required. When the student is no longer actively enrolled there is a six-month deferral period, with the presumption that the student has graduated and is seeking employment. If the student takes a semester, or two, or more off during their college career, those breaks will count towards that six-month grace period. This could mean the student is required to begin repayment of their loans before they have secured gainful employment. Gainful employment means consistent working with consistent pay as an employee or a 1099 contractor. A 1099 contractor is an independent worker that pays their employment taxes to the IRS themselves versus the employer deducting the taxes for an employee.

In addition to the federally funded Perkins Loan, Direct Subsidized, and Direct Unsubsidized student loans, there are private student loans through local and national banks and credit unions your student may qualify for. Each lender will have their own stipulations to the terms of repayment and interest rates. Your educational institution may provide a list of potential lenders, but they cannot advise you on the specifics of each and will refer you to the lender's website or financial loan officer. Private student loans can also be dictated by a student's credit score and current debt to income ratio (how much debt a student owes versus how much money they earn per year). Private loans may require a parental co-signer also. A student loan cosigner is typically a parent, guardian, spouse, relative, or friend of the student. To cosign, you need to meet general eligibility and credit requirements. The cosigner and student borrower share responsibility for loan repayment amount and terms.

Taking out a student loan does not instantly mean a student will be lumped into the statistics of people drowning in student loan debt, the student needs to be wise in their course of action pertaining to each individual loan. Students can falter or default on their loan which causes the interest to build and compound which will cause the total amount of repayment to escalate dramatically from what was originally agreed upon and borrowed. The best suggestion is the most aggressive suggestion, your student should start paying their student loans while they are still in school. Of course, this suggestion may sound "different" because the student is still working towards their education on a limited budget. Paying the minimum amount to cover the cost of interest is very smart. If the student can pay a bit more than the minimum amount the surplus money would go towards the principal balance (the original amount borrowed). While it does not sound like much, if the interest is being paid each month and some money paid towards principal, the total amount due will be significantly reduced cutting down the amount of time it takes to repay the loan in its entirety. The word principal is the initial size of a loan (the amount the borrower must repay).

As mentioned earlier student loans are one avenue to explore as funding, but there is a plethora of other options to fund a higher education as well. Most trade schools and vocational schools also offer grants based on financial need as well as earned merit-based scholarships. The federal government may provide grants based on perceived financial need (the criteria we discussed for student loans). Applying for grants and scholarships through local and national organizations is an optimal option that is cost effective as the student does not have to repay any money received. Most financial aid offices at various schools will have a list of currently recognized resources, as the list consistently grows and shrinks regularly.

In larger universities the departmental grants and scholarships are options in various majors such as Business Administration, Entrepreneurship or Pharmacy, just to name a few. Establishing and maintaining a high GPA, building a good rapport with instructors and advisors will be helpful in the search for funding. You could think of funding your child's education as your new part time job when looking for grants, scholarships, and other monies.

COLLEGE SUBMISSION APPLICATION

Your teen can apply for colleges and universities using the common application website (*https://www.commonapp.org/*). This is the quickest and most efficient way to apply to over 900 colleges and universities. There are several colleges that do not use this program, so you will want to check with the institution if you do not see them as an option when you create the profile. This user-friendly website walks your teen through submitting their credentials for consideration that could include entrance essays, letters of recommendations, certifications, and more depending on your teens field of study.

SCHOLARSHIPS

Apply, Apply, and APPLY some more! Scholarships are defined as a grant or payment made to support a student's education, awarded based on academic or other achievement. When applying for scholarships, please be mindful that the deadlines, amount of money awarded and criteria for the scholarship will vary. Some scholarships are renewable each year if you reapply and update your submission. Some scholarships are automatically renewed without any effort on your behalf. Setting aside time weekly or bi-weekly to search for or complete scholarship applications is mandatory to have the success you are looking for. During a student's high school career, their on-campus guidance counselor should also be able to provide scholarship listings and grant opportunities to them if requested. Your local schools will have connections with colleges that help streamline the process, but you must reach out to your high school guidance counselor for this assistance. It is not assumed that every graduating senior wants to continue their education, so it is a service provided when it is asked or sought after. Scholarships can be used at all accredited educational institutions in the United States. Accredited educational institutions are trade and vocational school, colleges, and universities. According to US News there are eight different types of scholarships.

Academic achievement- scholarships that are awarded to students that graduated as the top 3%-5%.

Community service- scholarships for students that give back to their communities by doing community service events.

Athletic achievement- scholarships that are offered for athletes that excel in their sport.

Unique hobbies or traits- scholarships for students that are creative, have interesting hobbies or have specific genetic traits such as a specific hair color.

Personal background- scholarships that focus to support traditionally underrepresented students.

Financial need- scholarships are focused helping those students that need financial support.

Family workplace- several employers offer scholarships for employees or dependents of their employees.

Military affiliation- all branches of the military offer servicemen and servicewomen along with their dependent's money for continuing education.

Listed below are a few links where you can search for scholarships. In no way are these the only resources to find scholarships, these are just a few suggestions to get you started. As an alert, no scholarship will require your debit or credit card information to apply. If the website or service you are using asks for a payment discontinue the process.

- *http://www.collegescholarships.org/financial-aid/*
- *https://scholarships360.org/scholarship/scholarships360-refer-a-friend-scholarship/*
- *https://tallo.com/scholarships360/*
- *https://www.fastweb.com/*
- *https://usagrantapplications.org/free-college-grants/index-v3.php*
- *https://www.financialaidfinder.com/category/scholarships/*

Regardless of how your student plans to fund their vocational, university, trade school, or college education financial stability is important. Financial stability could mean working while completing their education. Working while in school will catapult their professional career. Having real life employment experience is a tool your student can utilize during their interviews when they are seeking their "first real job" after graduation. When a potential employer looks over a resume of a new graduate, the student would be able to speak about their resourcefulness, time management skills while balancing high priority responsibilities proving to the employer, they understand the importance of organization, deadlines, and focus (goal setting). Your teen can speak about their work life balance, growth, and development opportunities because they have personally excelled at it.

There are several avenues you can explore for your high school student that can decrease the financial burden of building their career. Pell Grants and scholarships are the best solution that will not cause future turmoil with debt for your student. Pell grants are monies offered from the federal government that do **NOT** have to be repaid. Scholarships are the most popular forms of payment for trade or vocational school, college, or universities which also do not need to be paid back. A very important fact to remember is that each scholarship has different submission deadlines, qualifications, or criteria and value (dollar amounts) so, I encourage you to apply early, apply consistently and apply now.

According to the Pew Research Group 4/10 adults under the age of 30 have student loan debt. I personally have a crippling amount of student loan debt, due to my lack of effort with applying for scholarships and grants. I was a lazy student that did not do the leg work to find free money until my junior year of college. I did not see the value in looking for "free money" when I could just request more money from my lender. I lived on my student loans to support myself and my son. I was not receiving government assistance such as food stamps, child support, or cash assistance. I managed my bills such as day care, food, gas, car insurance, entertainment, clothing, rent, light, cellphone and water, each semester by maxing out my loan amounts. I paid my bills in advance and lived modestly with my paychecks. I managed to survive life's cuts or bruises, as I mounted a substantial amount of debt in return. If I would have utilized my free resources and had better spending habits, I would have avoided my current reality of debt. Scholarships exist for everyone. If you are left-handed, Native American, have a disability, or are a first-generation college student, grants are out there with your name on it. The more unique you are the more money is typically available. Your teen can start applying for some college scholarships at the age of 13. My son personally applied for Jack Kent Cooke Foundation scholarship for young scholars.

This scholarship pays for four years of education for your student:

- *https://www.jkcf.org/our-scholarships/*

A traditional full-time job may not be ideal for your student if the employer is not willing to be flexible with scheduling around their classes and other activities such as professional groups, organizations, or Greek life. Part-time employment may be ideal as they may be a little more flexible with different shift options. A flexible employment environment could be on campus employment with such positions as office assistant, bookstore clerk, or restaurant worker in the Student Union. Regardless of the route taken by your student, stress the importance of their academics over earning huge paychecks. Remind your student that employment is great, but their focus is finishing their education ultimately while maintaining a school/work balance.

COMMUNITY SERVICE & VOLUNTEER HOURS

Your teen will need to complete community service or volunteer hours for most of their scholarship's submissions. Your teen can volunteer at nonprofit or for-profit companies if it is approved by the school. In Florida, all community service and volunteer hours must be logged in Proffer (www.profferfish.com) to be counted towards their scholarship requirement. Once the data is inputted an email will be sent to the guidance counselor requesting, they approve the entries. After the guidance counselor approved the hours, the parent or guardian of the student will need to sign and approve the hours also. After both steps are completed the student will see their total approved hours on their profile screen.

Some school districts still use the paper submission method. Regardless to the method used, keep the lines of communication open with your teen's counselor to make sure they hours are logged and current.

REFERENCES

- *https://studentaid.gov/understand-aid/types/loans/interest-rates*
- *https://www.merriam-webster.com/dictionary/scholarship*

INTERNSHIPS

Dictionary.com says an internship is any official or formal program to provide practical experience for beginners in an occupation or profession; any period during which a beginner acquires experience in an occupation, profession, or pursuit. Most internship programs are structured to allow you to explore, within limits, the real day to day operations to see if you would like that field of study. Some internships are paid while others are not. The main goal of the internship is to gain exposure and experience.

Personally, speaking while in undergrad at Florida State, one of my internships was with a marketing firm in Tampa, Florida called SDot Marketing in 2008. I planned a fashion show to benefit the Warrick Dunn foundation. The show was a complete success!!! We raised enough money to outfit an entire room with furniture from the proceeds we raised from admission and donations. Organizing the show was extremely stressful, as the designers and models were very demanding and did not consider others wants or needs. During the planning phase, I switched designers twice, as their demands for stage time, extra recognition, and compensation was not the focus of the show. I realized the career choice of designer was too stressful and I would rather be a spectator to the magic not the curator. An internship is like test-driving a career choice, it almost guarantees you know what you will be getting yourself involved in after graduation. You can abandon ship on that career if necessary before you take too many classes toward the degree.

My second internship involved consistently traveling to various Karen Kane locations in Macy's department stores. I was a merchandising intern that traveled between Boca Raton, Florida to Aventura, Florida redoing floor displays with the latest release from the designer. As I visited each location, I quickly learned the customer in Boca differed from the Miami customer. I learned one ruler cannot measure the same distance, due to customer preferences, perceived bias, and needs. My internship involved creating art with clothes that helped women find themselves in their garments by loving their bodies. I was able to manage my day with personal shopping clients, department displays creations, and requesting shipment replenishments for hot sellers. I liked the organized chaos of fashion and retail, which led to my decision to begin my career in big box management.

Searching for an internship is rumored to be difficult, however, I assure you it is more difficult to settle into a career that you do not love. Searching for an internship paid or unpaid is not difficult. You can use your existing network of co-workers, friends, and family to get a solid start. Start speaking with people letting them know you are looking for an internship for your teen. They may know someone or they may be looking for an intern themselves. Let them know you are looking for exposure in the industry your teen choses. People genuinely want to help high school students figure out their place in life and would jump at the opportunity to be helpful. Paid internships will have a bigger pool of candidates to choose from, but do not let that deter your teen from applying. Internships will help your student stand out in comparison to their classmates when they are looking for employment.

EXPENSES: WHERE WILL THEY LAY THEIR HEAD?

Housing is another very important step to also discuss with your student. Where will your student live? It is imperative for them to keep living expenses as low as possible because other expenses such as car payment, auto insurance, phone, internet, entertainment, and grocery expenses are also factored into their monthly budget. Once they select a trade or vocational school, college, or university, start exploring the city to learn about the cost-of-living expenses, and commuting costs. How much are apartments? How much are efficiencies? Will they need a cosigner for their apartment? What are the financial requirements, is it the first month plus security deposit for securing an apartment? Finding an apartment in a new city can seem challenging if you do not know where to look. My suggestion is to grab the newspaper if you are old school. Apartment guidebooks can be found at local eateries as well. Your best friend for all research is "Google". Landlords and apartment complexes advertise their vacancies all over town and online to ensure they have enough exposure to keep their units filled each semester. If your student wants more freedom of their coming and going, an efficiency or an apartment may be the best living situation for them. If they have their own apartment, they will not have to conform to dorm curfews or spacing issues.

Discuss with your student the differences between living in a dorm (if they choose a college or a university) with a roommate in the same room 24 hours a day. Explain to them that their privacy is always shared. If the dorm room is single occupancy you can expect around 96 sq. ft., a double room measures 192 sq. ft and triple dorm room is about 368 sq. ft If your student likes to have their own space, quiet time, or their "privacy" a dorm may not be the best living option.

Regardless of personal preferences, please stress the importance of keeping their financials in mind and that compromise of their living situation is just that, a compromise with their goals in mind.

TO CAR OR NOT TO CAR

Will they have a car or use public transportation? If your student will not have a car and need to use public transportation, choosing an apartment that is a commutable distance is ideal. Commutable distance means you live as close as possible to your regular places you visit, so you can forego a vehicle and rely on public transportation, walking, or cycling.

Owning a vehicle means your student must consider insurance rates for their vehicle according to their credit score and area code. Insurance premiums range for various reasons such as age, city, credit score and marital status.

According to an article written by Rod Griffin for Propertycasualty360.com, he highlighted several aspects that could raise or decrease your student's premiums such as their current driving record, the vehicle make and model, location (city/state), level of desired coverage and protections, their credit score.

Chapter 4 - Debraca Russell MBA CPCC

COLLEGE IS NOT MY CHOICE

Trade school and vocational is worth its weight in gold

A vocational school is a post-secondary educational institution that provides technical training and skills for a specific job industry. One could say the birth of vocational school began in local high schools in America. High schools offered vocational training and courses such as home economics, wood shop, cosmetology, medical assistance, auto repair and business courses just to name a few. These courses were offered for free or with a small fee to ensure supplies were covered. The vocational course was considered an elective instead of a core class. The student could choose woodshop instead of physical education (gym). In the vocational course you were assigned homework and had regular exams to ensure you were absorbing the content being taught. The curriculum was no frills straight to the point content to ensure the student had a clear picture of an occupation in that field.

Growing up in Delray, I attended Carver Middle School where I personally took several vocational courses. I took woodshop as I had a true love for creating things with my hands. I was my mother's artsy child and loved the idea of creating something from nothing. My woodshop teacher was amazing for more than his woodwork. As a lifetime teacher and Father, Mr. Mitchell taught me more than sanding and gluing wood together. Mr. Mitchell taught me about perceptions and how my actions could reflect negatively or positively on my personal image. It took me several years to realize Mr. Mitchell was pouring into me something he felt I needed. Mr. Mitchell did not allow me to wear inappropriate clothing to his class. On several occasions, I questioned why he was riding about my clothes, Mr. Mitchell simply responded because it was his job to make sure

I always use your brain. If Mr. Mitchell saw me running down the hallway like a wild, rambunctious teen he would say, "Ms. Russell is that how a lady is supposed to act?" Mr. Mitchell quickly became the thorn in my side, until I realized that thorn was wrapped in sincere concern for my success. By God's grace, my thorn stayed close by until I graduated. My other vocational courses included home economics and typing.

My home economics teacher taught me how to cook basic meals, for the purpose of survival. She always mentioned how it was a struggle to please everyone in her home, so she cooked for her own taste and let everyone else season their food to their preference. This teacher taught me about foundations. Each meal is the foundation for energy to fuel the body. If I ate junk food every day, I would be unhealthy, and mentally sluggish. She drove home self-accountability surrounding health and food. She consistently warned how we can replace life situations with eating. I did not realize how much weight these words would hold until my freshman year of college. Freshman 15 was the 15lbs I gained from eating snickers bars, Tom's salt and vinegar chips for dinner, and the real college student delicacy ramen noodles. The routine of using measuring cups and leveling off flour are life lessons that still hold true. If you measure your amount of effort added in every situation the finished product will be one you would love to consume. If you throw random amounts of determination, planning, consistency, and effort at a situation, the outcome may not be as great as you wanted or envisioned. My biggest aha moment was I NEVER want to be a homemaker. Staying home cooking everyday breakfast, lunch, and dinner would be torture for me. I like the creativity of making meals from scratch with no recipe, but I know being a housewife is not my ideal existence. I like to cook for my family but hate the feeling of it being my main responsibility. I admire and respect home makers as their tolerance is impeccable. Balancing finances, errands, and regular maintenance of the home is not on my list of favorite things to do. The unsung heroes are homemakers! My last vocational course in middle school was typing. I thought I would love this course because my grandmother Emma Lee Gary always told me I would be a secretary in someone's office doing important work. I figured she knew something I did not, so I better get prepared for it.

In my typing course, I learned how to type and the importance of accuracy. My typing class was more than fingers on the keyboard, the course started out with 10 million handouts about finger placement, memorization, and hand/eye coordination. I assumed we would type Day 1, the reality was, we did not start typing until my teacher felt we were ready. She quizzed us on placement and why it linked directly to speed and accuracy. I remember trying to beat one of my classmates who could type 75 WPS (words per minute). I finally got to 45WPM and realized I did not want the title enough to practice the way she practiced and bowed out ungracefully (I was a sore loser). The life lesson I learned in typing was competitiveness is not enough to accomplish anything if you are not willing to put in the time and effort to learn the craft. I talked the talk and refused to walk the walk. I only practiced my typing in class and I never stayed after school when my classmate stayed every day. My social life was full and I refused to sacrifice having fun to polish my typing skills. Learning and experiencing home economics, typing, and woodshop in middle school taught me several things about myself at an early age. Life lessons will be the attainable fruit for your student in different parts of life. My suggestion as a parent is to be there emotionally as a sounding board, cheerleader, and mirror for your child.

Currently budget cuts have caused several high schools to lose their funding for these amazing vocational programs, which in turn leaves the student to secure this knowledge after high school or through extracurricular activities. There are hundreds of trades that would enable your student to make over 40k per year. Searching for a financially lucrative trade could seem like a daunting task, but this book is your guide to making it easier. As I previously stated, our teens depend on us to help them navigate the unknown waters of life, their education, and searching for a career. Let's remove the component of fear and replace it with tools to succeed. The Occupational handbook *https://www.bls.gov/* is an amazing tool where you can search using different filters to find career options that would interest your teen. Your student has unlimited access to knowledge by using this free tool. No career path is unavailable to your student if they are willing to use their curiosity to discover it!

Keep in mind, vocational school is not a free education. You will need to consider the cost of the education acquired with the potential for gainful employment. Research the field your teen is interested in pursuing with the demand for employees. Please be mindful about the reality of supply and demand. If your student gets an education in basket weaving, what is the demand for basket weavers in California, what about Florida, let's consider Virginia? You can check the demand in your city or state using job board websites such as Indeed, LinkedIn, or Glassdoor.com. You want to ensure there is a genuine demand for the trade before you guide your student to it. In no way do you want to dampen the light of excitement, you want to give your student realistic information so they can gauge the outcome of their career. Paying for vocational training with scholarships or grants is a good way to avoid debt. Most vocational schools have their own scholarship process as well, so please do not assume all scholarships can be used at every institution. Seeking guidance from the vocational school is the only way to ensure you have concrete information to help your student with paying for their education. Vocational schools are a clever alternative to a formal education.

There is a common phrase that I was taught in my freshman year of college by the SPC101 (Speech class) instructor, while I no longer remember his name, I still remember him saying. KISS-Keep it Simple Stupid. This adage holds true in most circumstances, but never more so than when trying to get through your secondary education and while balancing work life, home life, and school life - Allison Nasche.

Your student can finish a trade or vocational training program in as little as nine months depending on the career field. If your student is curious about a field acquiring a trade in the field could be a safe step to "test" the waters. For example, your daughter says she wants to be a nurse, but is squeamish with the sight of blood, becoming a medical assistant would give her a true snapshot of life as a nurse. While pursuing her classes your student will see if she is cut out to be a nurse. She would see the shifts, routine of caring for patients and the responsibility of being a medical professional. Careers that are started with your vocational career are as lucrative as a college education. Remember your number one goal is to keep your teen focused on positive transition. Do not be boxed into anyone's goal for your teen. Your teen's future is theirs to navigate as you support them.

CAREER OPTIONS & ANNUAL SALARIES

Web Developer 82k	Diagnostic Medical Sonographer 75k	Respiratory Therapist 63k
Nuclear Medicine Technologist 80k	Aircraft Mechanic or Service Technician 67k	Engineering Technician 65k
Magnetic Resonance Imaging Technologist 74k	Radiologic Technologist 63k	Captain, Mate or Pilot of Water Vessels 87k
Physical Therapy Assistant 58k	Occupational Therapist Assistant 61k	Funeral Service Manager 95k
Legal Assistant or Paralegal 55k	Radiation Therapist 91k	Geological or Petroleum Technician 60k

LET'S GET TO WORK!

In the early 1920's manual labor was a field of blood, sweat and tears; railroad manufacturing, farming, and factory workers all endured harsh conditions to create revenue for their families. Technology has changed the face of manufacturing in the 21st century. Manufacturing today involves computers, machines, and plush salaries. Several trades involve no physical exertion, only "brain power". What career path do they want to pursue? These loaded questions are ones only your teen on the brink of adulthood can answer. Some high school students are still deciding what they want for lunch, let alone deciding what they will do for the next 20 or 30 years of their life. Allow your teen to explore career paths. Never make your teen think their dream is inferior to another person's dream of college or the military. Everyone has a different vision for their future, as a parent our biggest opportunity, and hurdle is support without condemning their decisions.

If your teen is not interested in getting a degree or secondary education from a vocational or technical school, you can help them pursue jobs that offer them on the job training or an apprenticeship program. According to the Department of Labor, apprenticeships combine paid on-the-job training with classroom instruction to prepare workers for highly skilled careers. A few great places to start your search would be at Apprenticeship.gov or the US Department of Labor. These two websites can be the compass to a brand-new future potentially debt free! The two websites *https://www.apprenticeship.gov/employers/industry-recognized-apprenticeship-program*   or *https://www.dol.gov/apprenticeship/* allow you to set up filters by city, state, company name, or occupation.

APPRENTICESHIP

Youth Apprenticeship programs are available to students after they turn 16. After graduation they would be eligible for an adult apprenticeship. Your teen can explore this option instead of vocational or trade schools. An apprentice is a person who is learning a trade from a skilled employer. Most apprenticeship programs pay the student a fraction of the wage of an entry level employee. Every apprenticeship program has requirements of hours worked and successful completion of training modules. Once the apprentice has passed all the requirements, they are considered entry level and paid according to their training in that field. Follow the link to search for programs registered with the Department of Education (*http://www.fldoe.org/academics/career-adult-edu/apprenticeship-programs/*). A few careers your student can explore in the youth apprenticeship program are Carpenter, Plumber, Electrician, Ironworker, Pipefitter, Bricklayer, HVAC, Maintenance repairer, Childcare development specialist. The adult apprenticeship program offers over 25 different paths such as Electronics Technician, Community Health Worker, Welder, Sheet metal worker, and machinist.

References

- *https://www.bls.gov/ooh/occupation-finder.htm?pay=&education =&training=&newjobs=&growth=&submit=GO*
- *Internshipprograms.com*

UNSKILLED EMPLOYMENT

Careers that are in high demand may offer a higher salary versus a career field that is saturated (meaning has more available workers than the need in that area). Unskilled labor jobs or occupations are typically more physically demanding careers that can be more difficult to get into because the pool of candidates is saturated with potential. Some high school seniors pursue a career such as a warehouse worker, forklift operator, shipping, and receiving clerk because the work is not complex, and the schedules are consistent. Unfortunately, those types of unskilled jobs will have several hundred candidates applying every day. For example, I worked as a HR Assistant for a trucking company where we had warehouse workers work around the clock. I remember opening a requisition (job posting) for a 3rd shift warehouse worker for $11.00 per hour and we received over 500 submissions in one month. Trying to review 500 submissions for one job opening is difficult, I guess the better word would be impossible. I then realized I needed to be more specific with setting the criteria for applicants. I was able to ask for the pink unicorn on every job we offered because we had great benefits, a good working environment, and an active management team. The pink unicorn is the "perfect employee", the skills you wish every employee had. This is the normal situation for non-skilled positions, as the employment market is consistently turning out new non-skilled workers.

Most employers will consider certain variables when selecting who to call for an interview and eventually hire. The employer could evaluate the current staff and environment to see what "he or she needs" regarding personnel. Do they have an age mature work environment and need a worker bee that will take direction without any suggestions or objections? Do they want someone with previous experience or certifications to round off their already experienced work environment? What are they willing to pay a new employee with experience? Do they have "quality" training programs that will allow them to hire someone with no experience? These are a few of the possible questions hiring managers will consider when they are looking for the "ideal candidate".

Parents there is no guaranteed way to know what an employer is looking for unless you ask. Please do not let someone promise they can get your teen an interview unless they know the person doing the hiring personally. The inside connection is a great way to get your ROCKSTAR teen a job, but it is not the only way. If you and your student want more life skills exposure, employment may not be the best avenue to take right away. The United States military may be your solution. In the next chapter we will discuss branches of the military, enlistment, and scholarships.

Chapter 5 - Debraca Russell MBA CPCC

THE MILITARY: AT YOUR SERVICE

If your student is interested in the military, getting them involved in ROTC in high school would allow them to explore the similarities. Your teen can enroll their freshmen, sophomore, or junior year of high school. When making your course selections they would choose JROTC as their elective. My oldest sister joined JROTC in high school and loved it. She mentioned one of the best benefits, in her opinion, was getting into all the games for free and performing at the parades. She learned how to handle a firearm safely, personal accountability, and discipline just to name a few. She decided not to enlist in the military after graduation, she pursued a career in the medical field. According to Navy Capt. James Boyer, citizenship, leadership, character, and community service are the core tenets of high school Junior Reserve Officer Training Corps programs, or JROTC. Those values are at the heart of the JROTC Cadet Creed that emphasizes working to better the cadet's family, school, and country. The goal of JROTC programs, experts say, is good citizenship. "Students get a sense of home, a greater sense of family, of unity," says retired Navy Capt. James Boyer, senior naval science officer and Navy JROTC instructor at Spring High School in Texas. Students learn the values of citizenship, he says, by doing the right thing daily.

Once your student has decided they want to pursue a military career, they should inform their guidance counselor of their intentions. The counselor can help your student not miss out on information or services the school or community may provide such as meet and greets when Recruiters come on campus. Another option is to follow the link (*https://www.officialasvab.com/*) and contact your local Recruiter. Prior to scheduling the ASVAB exam for your teen, the Recruiter will get to know your student to ensure they qualify. After the preliminary interview, the Recruiter will schedule for your teen to take the exam. Remember you can ask your Recruiter any questions you have, they are a resource of things to come in the process. Every Recruiter is a service member. They can share their experience, lessons, and aspirations with your student. The Recruiter can help your teen understand the purpose of the ASVAB exam and how it relates to their future assignment.

The Armed Services Vocational Aptitude Battery (ASVAB) is a multiple-aptitude battery that measures developed abilities and helps predict future academic and occupational success in the military. It is administered annually to more than one million military applicants, high school, and post-secondary students according to the website (*https://www.officialasvab.com/*).

Most people do not know, I considered a life of service in the United States Military. I was approached at school by a Recruiter from the National Guard. The promise of a steady paycheck, free morning workouts, and a gang of friends made me believe being a servicemember was the best option for me. I did not do my due diligence to find out the free morning workouts meant 4am training for hours or that the gang of friends meant living in close quarters (dorm style) for basic training. Once I realized this was not going to be a nonstop option to vacation wherever I wanted in the world, I decided not to enlist. After some thought I knew I was not military material as the idea of war made me cringe and sweating was not my favorite pastime activity.

I am sure you have heard several myths about military life. Anyone that enlists will come home crazy. Everyone comes home disabled with some wound that never heals. They are abusing people mentally in the military. You will be experimented on with chemicals unknown to the world by "Doctors". I know several service members that have returned home from war, routine service, and none of those myths mentioned are true.

Testimonial #1: Growing up in an awkward family with unspoken regrets, this airman knew he wanted a way out of his bleak reality as soon as possible. He enlisted because his career as a Taco Bell manager did not seem as promising as he initially thought it would be. He wanted to explore more than the walls of his city in Florida. He was curious of how others were prospering and wanted in. He gave the military a "try" to see what would happen. Once he enlisted, he fell in love with the challenge of succeeding. He pushed himself and consumed knowledge he did not know he yearned for. After his 20 years of service, he is a successful IT engineer, a devoted mentor, aspiring activist, and proud Father of two. During his service to our nations, he developed a passion for serving others. He volunteers as a mentor, to feed the homeless, donates to charities and makes his voice heard in today's society as a parent and a human.

Testimonial #2: Born in Chester, Pennsylvania, this Major grew up near the port. He found his love for the military because they built Aircraft carriers in his hometown. Wanting to leave this crime and poverty-stricken city he enlisted in the United States Army. He knew this opportunity would help him get past his initial failure as a college student. He acquired his training to become a commercial truck driver in the Army. After his initial service in the Army, he entered a military college where he earned his commission as a Second Lieutenant and transferred to earn his Bachelor of Art from American University. Unfortunately, after college while completing his officer training he was decommissioned. He did not give up and enlisted in the Air Force which led him back to regain his commission and retire as a Major. He is a proud retired Army Major, has three beautiful children and lives a life of service by assisting retired veterans with education, employment, and stabilizing housing. This lifetime leader knows his greatest legacy is how he helps and promotes his other servicemen and women.

My suggestion is that you do your research by contacting all the branches to have a clear picture of what each branch offer and how this will resonate with your student's goals, dreams, and believed aspirations for their military career. Speaking with current or recently retired service members that you know personally is another way to ensure you are getting the details you want and need. If someone is currently pursuing the career path your student wants to pursue, it never hurts to ask them their details of what they did and how they did it. In no way does that guarantee your student will have the exact experience or outcome, but it does give your student a skeleton of possibilities to explore.

YOUR MILITARY DEDICATION IS SUPPORTED BY A FREE EDUCATION

Our military service men and women are the foundation of our culture so keeping them in the best shape mentally, spiritually, and financially is a sincere effort of our culture. Several states offer free education for military services members and their children(*https:// militarybenefits.info/states-offer-free-tuition-veterans/*) to ensure education is never a barrier to their success. Subscribe to the military. com website where each branch of the military is highlighted. The website answers questions about requirements for tuition reimbursement, G.I Bill guidelines, and scholarships. Listed below are a few colleges and universities that offer a free education for service members and their families.

ALABAMA FREE COLLEGE TUITION FOR VETERANS

Alabama's public two-year and four-year postsecondary technical colleges, community colleges, and junior colleges may waive tuition and fees for recipients of the Purple Heart Medal for undergraduate studies.

ARIZONA FREE COLLEGE TUITION FOR VETERANS

The Arizona Purple Heart Tuition Waiver provides qualifying Post 9/11 veterans with tuition-free education at any public state university or community college. To qualify, you must be a resident veteran who has at least a 50% VA disability and received a Purple Heart medal. You must also be accepted to the school you would like to attend.

CONNECTICUT FREE COLLEGE TUITION FOR VETERANS

Connecticut offers college tuition waivers for qualified veterans attending any state university or one of the 12 Connecticut Community College/Technical Colleges. This benefit is only applicable for tuition expenses for undergraduate and graduate programs and excludes course fees, books, parking, and room/board.

FLORIDA FREE COLLEGE TUITION FOR VETERANS

The State of Florida offers qualifying veterans' free undergraduate tuition at state universities and community colleges (excludes textbooks, housing, and food). This Florida state military educational benefit is intended for Florida residents who have received the Purple Heart or one of the following decorations:

- *Medal of Honor*
- *Navy Cross/Air Force Cross/Distinguished Service Cross*
- *Distinguished Service Medal with Combat V*
- *Silver Star Legion of Merit with Combat V*
- *Distinguished Flying Cross*
- *Bronze Star with Combat V*

ILLINOIS FREE COLLEGE TUITION FOR VETERANS

The Illinois Veteran Grant Program offers Illinois veterans free tuition and the payment of selected fees at all Illinois state colleges and universities.

To qualify, you must:

- *have a minimum of one year of service*
- *have an honorable discharge*
- *have Illinois listed as the home of record*
- *return to Illinois within six months of leaving military service*

INDIANA FREE COLLEGE TUITION FOR VETERANS

The State of Indiana offers free tuition up to 124 credit hours in a state-sponsored college/university for qualifying veterans who received the Purple Heart, entered active duty with a permanent home address in Indiana, and was honorably discharged.

MARYLAND FREE COLLEGE TUITION
FOR VETERANS

Maryland's Edward T. Conroy Memorial Scholarship provides tuition assistance and other educational expenses to veterans attending an institution of higher learning in the State of Maryland.

You must be a veteran who suffers, as a direct result of military service, a disability of 25 percent or greater and has exhausted or is no longer eligible for federal veterans educational benefits a POW/MIA of the Vietnam Conflict

MASSACHUSETTS FREE COLLEGE TUITION
FOR VETERANS

The Commonwealth of Massachusetts offers a tuition waiver to all veterans and active duty members who are permanent and legal residents of Massachusetts. This waiver is good for any Massachusetts state or community college or university campus.

MONTANA FREE COLLEGE TUITION
FOR VETERANS

The State of Montana offers qualifying veterans' free tuition at state schools for up to 12 semesters. The veteran must be classified as an in-state resident and have already used up all available federal GI Bill benefits.

To qualify for free tuition, you must have been honorably discharged, and performed military service in an approved war zone or campaign.

NEW MEXICO FREE COLLEGE TUITION
FOR VETERANS

Wartime Veteran Scholarship Fund

The Wartime Veteran Scholarship Fund is available for any veteran who has served in combat since 1990 and who has exhausted all available federal GI Bill benefits. The scholarship is available on a first-come, first-served basis while funds last. This program is for state-funded schools and is for tuition and book expenses for undergraduate and graduate work only.

You qualify if you have been a New Mexico resident for a minimum of 10 years, and awarded the Southwest Asia Service Medal, Global War on Terrorism Expeditionary Medal, Iraq Campaign Medal, Afghanistan Campaign Medal, or "any other medal issued for service in support of any other approved US Military campaign or armed conflict since 1990.

RHODE ISLAND FREE COLLEGE TUITION FOR VETERANS

Rhode Island offers free tuition at Rhode Island public colleges and universities for disabled veterans. Veterans must be rated between 10% and 100% VA disabled due to military service, and permanent residents of Rhode Island. Applicants must also apply for and use federal financial aid before any state assistance is applied.

TENNESSEE FREE COLLEGE TUITION FOR VETERANS

The Helping Heroes Grant awards up to $1,000 per semester for up to eight full semesters for honorably discharged veterans and service members in Tennessee. Current & former reserve or national guard members called into active duty are also eligible. Qualified members must have been a Tennessee resident for one year prior to completing the grant application. The amount of financial aid you may qualify for is dependent on the nature of your military service. Veterans must also complete 12 or more credits each semester. The Helping Heroes Grant is awarded to on average 375 veterans per year. Applicants must not hold a baccalaureate degree and be enrolled in a 2- or 4-year postsecondary institution.

TEXAS FREE COLLEGE TUITION FOR VETERANS

The State of Texas offers benefits through the Hazelwood Act. This benefit provides qualified veterans an education benefit of up to 150 hours of tuition exemption, including most fee charges, at public institutions of higher education in Texas. The exemption does not include living expenses, books, or supply fees.

To qualify, you must have served 181 days or more on active duty, received an honorable discharge, and have no federal Veteran's education benefits remaining, and met residency requirements

UTAH FREE COLLEGE TUITION FOR VETERANS

The State of Utah offers multiple programs to qualifying veterans and military dependents.

State of Utah Purple Heart Tuition Waiver

Purple Heart recipients can apply for a tuition waiver at all state-sponsored/public colleges/universities in Utah. This tuition benefit is good for undergrad and graduate work. Purple Heart documentation is required to apply for this benefit.

Scott Lundell Military Survivors Tuition Waiver

Surviving dependents of service members killed in action on or after September 11, 2001, are eligible to apply for a tuition waiver good at state-supported schools. at state schools. According to the State of Utah, qualifying conditions for applicants include the following:

Dependent may not have already completed a course of studies leading to an undergraduate degree.

Dependents may only utilize the waiver for courses that are applicable toward the degree or certificate requirements of the program in which the dependent is enrolled.

Dependents may not be excluded from the waiver if the dependent has previously taken courses at or has been awarded credit by a state institution of higher education.

Utah Veterans Tuition Gap Program

WASHINGTON FREE COLLEGE TUITION FOR VETERANS

Washington State colleges establish their own waiver programs for eligible resident veterans. Washington State law allows a waiver for qualified veterans up to the full amount of tuition and fees and participating schools.

How to apply to each college or university establishes and operates its own veteran's waiver program, so it is best to get in touch with the college or university you plan to attend for details on their program.

WEST VIRGINIA FREE COLLEGE TUITION FOR VETERANS

The Medal of Honor and Andrew J. Trail Purple Heart Recipient Tuition Waiver provides free tuition and mandatory fees for residents who have been awarded the Medal of Honor or Purple Heart. The waiver is good for 8 semesters of free tuition at all West Virginia public institutions of higher education.

How to apply, visit the Financial Aid Office at the institution you are attending.

WISCONSIN FREE COLLEGE TUITION FOR VETERANS

Wisconsin offers a State GI Bill that enables qualifying Wisconsin veterans to attend public postsecondary educational institutions tuition-free. The program offers full waivers for tuition and fees up to 8 semesters or 128 credit hours. This program can be used for undergraduate, master's, or doctoral degrees at the University of

Wisconsin or Wisconsin Technical College institution (any location) and in any degree program.

To qualify, you must: have received an honorable discharge, and met all military service and residency requirements.

To apply, visit the Wisconsin Department of Veterans Affairs online portal and create an account. You will be asked to enter all required information and upload supporting documents that prove your eligibility. If you are eligible, you will get a certificate of eligibility. You will need the certificate to apply for the Wisconsin GI Bill though your institution.

WYOMING FREE COLLEGE TUITION FOR VETERANS

Wyoming offers free tuition and fees for qualifying resident veterans. The tuition waiver is good for 8 semesters over 8 years while attending the University of Wyoming or Wyoming community colleges. You qualify for the free tuition if you: served in Vietnam between August 5, 1964, and May 7, 1975, and received the Vietnam Service Medal, or are an overseas combat veteran who was honorably discharged and awarded the armed forces expeditionary medal or other authorized service or campaign medal indicating service to the United States in any armed conflict in a foreign country.

As a service men and women your student would be eligible for educational assistance which means a free education with their GI Bill grant, home loan assistance when they are ready to establish a permanent place of residence, and free healthcare for life through the Veteran Hospital in their area. Every branch of the military is known to have amazing benefits and top of the line training programs. Again, your Recruiter will highlight all the benefits of becoming a military man or woman.

REFERENCES

- *https://www.officialasvab.com/*
- *https://militarybenefits.info/states-offer-free-tuition-veterans/)*

- *https://www.military.com/education/money-for-school/army-tuition-assistance.html*
- *https://www.navycollege.navy.mil/sailors/tuition-assistance-ncpace.htm*

Transitioning from our military conversation to our next contributing author, we wanted to add some sauce to make sure this book was dripping. Okay, I know that was horrible to say on all levels, but remember your teen needs you to speak their language. This next and final chapter gets "saucy" learning about money and how your teen can use it or lose it from financial guru, Mr. Javed Morgan.

The reason I chose Mr. Morgan to speak about this topic was his practical, knowledgeable approach to financial literacy, and execution. Javed is an authentic individual that gives proven facts and tips to financial growth through literacy. I have trusted Javed personally with my own finances for years and will continue to do business with him because of his ethics and integrity.

Mr. Morgan is a native of Jamaica that migrated to the United States at the age of 11 to Tampa, Florida. No stranger to hard work, determination, and goals, Javed excelled as an athlete and a student. As a graduate from the University of Central Florida, with a Bachelor of Science in Restaurant Management, Javed set his mind of another goal. This goal was something wild and unhinged, this goal was something that scares most to even consider, the goal was turning dreams of financial stability into his reality. When Javed was 16, he watched a documentary featuring Warren Buffet that exposed him to how to build, protect and pass wealth along with generational wealth building strategies. Javed has a passion for financial literacy, so I knew he was the perfect person for this next chapter.

Chapter 6 - Javed Morgan

MAKE THE MONEY, DON'T LET THE MONEY MAKE YOU

You have gone through Middle School and made some friends here and there. You are now in high school, taken all kinds of classes and still no research on Money! You start to wonder about some of the classes you are taking. Will I really need any of this information like algebra and geometry in my real life? Now, it is after graduation, you are at the age where you can make your own decisions and you don't have to abide by those strict rules that your parents set for you while you were under their roof; that means you can spend your money whenever and however you choose.

Imagine after graduating from high school your son or daughter will need help moving into their first dorm, apartment, or simply managing their money while staying at home. They have a good job working 30 hours a week while attending college on a full-time basis. Keep in mind this entire time no one has spoken to them about money or how to manage money. After the first few weeks they will receive a nice lump sum of cash in the form of Financial Aid. And guess what? Your student could blow through those funds within a matter of weeks on frivolous stuff like video games, hanging out, and meals they've dreamed about for weeks. Now their bills are due, you look up to check on their finances, and see their bank account says NSF (non-sufficient funds)! You're now asking yourself all sorts of questions. What happened here? Where did all my money go? What did they spend their money on? Wait, what did I teach him or her about money? For most Americans, this story is all but too familiar. Unfortunately, many adults in life have had to learn about budgeting through the school of hard knocks.

Most teens do not truly grasp the concept of budgeting, resulting in a whopping 76% of Americans living paycheck to paycheck. Why? Most Americans make good money; however, their spending habits are extremely dangerous. Many have never been taught how to control emotional urges and impulses that push them into the vicious cycle of living paycheck to paycheck.

Have you ever seen a hamster on a hamster wheel running and going nowhere? This exemplifies the paycheck-to-paycheck sequence. So how can this epidemic be solved? What are some things that can be done to prevent bad budgeting traits over a lifetime? I am glad you asked! Before I share a few concepts and ideas with you I would like to share a fundamental concept about money.

Firstly, I would like to introduce a financial concept developed by a gray hair guy by the name of Albert Einstein. This concept is the 8th wonder of the world. Once you understand it, it will change your life, your family's life, and the way you look at money forever!

The Rule of 72 is a Mathematical shortcut that tells you how long the money you save will double or how fast your debts can double. Anyone who lends money, has used this rule to work against those that borrow money. Simply take whatever interest rate you are being charged and divide that into the 72. That will tell you the number of years it will take for your money to double.

For example: 72 ÷ 1% (Interest Rate) = 72 years for your money to double. 72 ÷ 6 = 12 years so on and so forth. In essence the higher the rate of return one can earn, the more years you give your money the chance to double and the lower rate of return you earn the longer it will take for your money to double and less years. 72 ÷ 17% = 4.2 years for your debt to double. With 17% being the average credit card interest rate in America. That said, 1% is NOT the average interest rates that Banks give their clients in a Savings account; it's actually less, .09% to be exact. So, if you are saving money in a Bank account your money will not double until 800 years. Yes, you read that correctly, it will take 800 years for your money to double at the Bank.

For example, you have $10,000 at the Bank, for it to double to $20,000 it will take 800 years. When you do the math, you will see that 72 ÷ .09% = 800. At the same token they lend you your own money back in the form of Auto, Mortgage, Personal Loans, Credit Cards, and charge anywhere from 4% to 30% interest to do so. Why is all this important? The more you understand how to properly budget, you will then be able to allocate your funds to different wealth building strategies that will enable you to receive higher rates of return. This means your money is working for you and not against you.

As a young adult the lack of budgeting skills can cause your graduate to have more months at the end of your checks than you have money. The first budgeting skill one should master: Have financial goals. Where would I like to be 1, 3, 5, or 10 years from now? How much money do I want to have invested in my retirement account? How much money do I want to have in my bank account liquid? Liquid bank accounts are those you can get your money out of quickly and easily. A variety of bank accounts are liquid assets -- unlike other assets that you cannot readily convert to cash, such as real estate. Liquid bank accounts include checking accounts, money market accounts, and savings accounts.

Having financial goals keeps us focused and on target, it helps the reticular activating system part of the brain to find ways to accomplish those things that you have set before it subconsciously. Your financial goals that your graduate set in place must be realistic. Why? You want to feel as though your goals are achievable.

For example, if you are single and only make $45,000 per year; a simple financial goal would be to save $6,000 for the year and pay down debt. Creating a goal of saving 10,000 in one year is not a realistic goal when you have other ancillary bills that also need your attention. This will reduce your excitement and decrease your spirits which could cause you to give up on pursuing your financial goals. Help your son or daughter set financial goals, encourage them to look at them daily and repeat them to themselves morning, afternoon, and night before they go to bed.

After they have set their financial goals, they need to look at how much net income they bring home each month. Net Income is the money that is distributed into your bank account via direct deposit or way of paper check in your hands weekly or bi-weekly. Once you have analyzed how much net income you take home, you should now list every bill that you have.

Bills are expenses such as rent, light bill, tithes, water bill, car note, car insurance, cable, Netflix/ HULU subscription, apple music, eating out, and fun money, just to name a few. Add the total amount up, subtract this from your net income and see if you break even, in the negatives, or if you have a surplus at the end.

If you are in the negative, then you have some bills or things you do in your leisure time to cut back on or give up all together. If you have broken even, consider adding a side hustle in the form of a business, this way you can still reach some of the financial goals that you have for yourself. If your graduate has a surplus of money, these are the funds that could be used to help save, decrease debts, and/or build an emergency fund. An emergency fund is money saved for the unplanned situations that happen in life like, loss of employment, or car repairs.

After they have made their financial goals and you have helped them configure a budget by listing all their bills. Now what? Next, you want to tell the money where to go. This means they will have to be deliberate where the funds are going. There is a saying: "tell your money where to go or at the end of each month or you'll wonder where my money went?" For each of your bills that are listed they can either use the "cash method" this means you get envelopes for all your bills, write out the amount due each month. Each paycheck you disperse the necessary funds to the different envelopes. The cash method takes a little bit of work, but this is what it takes to really get your finances under control and avoid the trap of paycheck to paycheck that I spoke about earlier.

Make a Budget

Use this worksheet to see how much money you spend this month. Then, use this month's information to help you plan next month's budget.

Some bills are monthly and some come less often. If you have an expense that does not occur every month, put it in the "Other expenses this month" category.

MONTH _____ YEAR _____

My income this month

Income	Monthly total
Paychecks (salary after taxes, benefits, and check cashing fees)	$
Other income (after taxes) for example: child support	$
Total monthly income	$ 0.00

Income

My expenses this month

	Expenses	Monthly total
HOUSING	Rent or mortgage	$
	Renter's insurance or homeowner's insurance	$
	Utilities (like electricity and gas)	$
	Internet, cable, and phones	$
	Other housing expenses (like property taxes)	$
FOOD	Groceries and household supplies	$
	Meals out	$
	Other food expenses	$
TRANSPORTATION	Public transportation and taxis	$
	Gas for car	$
	Parking and tolls	$
	Car maintenance (like oil changes)	$
	Car insurance	$
	Car loan	$
	Other transportation expenses	$

Make a Budget

	Expenses	Monthly total
HEALTH	Medicine	$
	Health insurance	$
	Other health expenses (like doctors' appointments and eyeglasses)	$
PERSONAL AND FAMILY	Child care	$
	Child support	$
	Money given or sent to family	$
	Clothing and shoes	$
	Laundry	$
	Donations	$
	Entertainment (like movies and amusement parks)	$
	Other personal or family expenses (like beauty care)	$
FINANCE	Fees for cashier's checks and money transfers	$
	Prepaid cards and phone cards	$
	Bank or credit card fees	$
	Other fees	$
OTHER	School costs (like supplies, tuition, student loans)	$
	Other payments (like credit cards and savings)	$
	Other expenses this month	$
	Total monthly expenses	$ 0.00
		Expenses

$ 0.00   − $ 0.00   = $ 0.00

Income   **Expenses**

Maybe your income is more than your expenses. You have money left to save or spend.

Maybe your expenses are more than your income. Look at your budget to find expenses to cut.

The next step could be them creating an automated bank account for their bills. This will help them focus on other areas to improve upon financially speaking. To do this, they will need to make sure they know the total amount for all bills going out of your household each month. You can go to your HR Department and have your weekly or bi-weekly check disperse into two separate accounts, or you can personally divide up amounts once deposited into your main bank account to the billing account. Setting up EFT (electronic fund transfers) is another way of worrying about one less thing each month. Your teen can set it up and monitor the account one to two times a month to make sure the various companies are taking out the allotted amount they should be. This method would prevent them from falling behind on any of their bills avoiding bills being past due or late fees.

That leads me to my next example: We struggle when it comes to budgeting. What can we do? If you have multiple credit cards or personal loans you should attack the credit card with the highest interest rate first not the one that is the highest balance. The card with the highest interest can be your greatest enemy! Remember that "Rule of 72?" that comes into effect here which is why you want to be laser focused on that card or loan with the highest interest.

Let us recap. Your student needs to establish their financial goals, list all their bills on paper, tell the money where to go, and lastly, they need to invest their surplus and use that to build to complete some of those financial goals they have set for themselves. Having a budget is crucial to financial survival. It is in my professional opinion one of the things that separate the wealthy from the poor. Keeping your teen focused with text reminders every few months is a great key. Remember to be on their side and ready to help when they need it. The direct link from money is your occupation. The next chapter is about employment realities for your student.

Hello again, I am Debraca Russell and I am a certified career coach. The hardest question for anyone to answer is "Who am I and what do I want to do in my career"?

Chapter 7 - Debraca Russell MBA CPCC

LET'S GET YOU HIRED

In this book the belief is echoed, securing employment for your student does not have to be impossible! I repeat, teenagers can have fruitful employment opportunities if you strategically plan for it. Planning for your teen to have a job or begin a career involves open minds and clear communication. The conversation is the first step in understanding what makes your teen tick. If my son or daughter likes computers, the job should have technology in it. If your son or daughter likes being around children, teaching children, mentoring, or growth a rewarding job could be at a daycare.

Once a career path, occupation, or idea is identified do a search to identify companies that have the type of employment they want. For example, if your student wants to pursue something in the medical field, check the blood banks, your primary care physician office, and your network of friends to see who would let your child shadow or volunteer for a few hours a week. This step helps your adolescent understand what it means to work in this career field seriously.

Your teen will need a resume and possibly a cover letter when applying for employment. As a Certified Career Coach, I teach my clients to be prepared so they do not have to get prepared later. Being prepared is as simple as investing in yourself. Resume writers and Career Coaches can be an investment that you question due to the cost. I understand the mental struggle of paying hundreds of dollars for a document that does not "GUARANTEE" you will get the job. I ask you to imagine NOT investing in a quality document and think of how long it will take to secure the interview and job. Giving you the nuggets of employment is the goal for this chapter.

How can we prevent your graduate from being left on the sideline as unemployed?

RESUME RULES FROM THE FOUNDER OF AGAPE CAREER COUNSELING GROUP

1. Do you put your date of birth, social security number, physical living address, or unprofessional email address on the resume. An unprofessional email address will lead your student to be judged on personal bias and generational prejudices just to name a few. Keeping the email address neutral to their name Debraca.Russell@blahblahblah.com is best. If their name is not an available email address try adding a numeric to the words.

2. Do not you use vague language on the resume. Make all the statements and sentences specific and to the point under each heading. If you student held a leadership position, use it as an accomplishment and identify what type of leader they are. LinkedIn has an article (*https://www.indeed.com/career-advice/career-development/10-common-leadership-styles*) that highlights what each style is and how it is fruitful in various work environments. The resume should not be written like a list of tasks accomplished. The resume needs to show how your student made a difference in the work environment from their accomplishments.

3. List any accomplishments your students achieve under a heading "Recognitions & Accomplishments". This heading should be .right underneath your student's name, contact phone number and email address (professional email addresses only). Do not put their birthday in the email address (Russell2003@yahoo.com tells me you were born and 2003). Reverse age discrimination happens when a younger person is not considered for employment due to their age. Listing their accomplishments informs the hiring manager, HR Recruiter or Talent Acquisition Recruiter that your student is effective in their position and is a ROCKSTAR they would consider interviewing.

4. Do not put the phrase, "reference available upon request" on your resume. The reader, hiring manager, or recruiter already knows you will furnish references when they request them. Using the phrase is a space stealer that does not help your student get an interview. Do not add tables or charts to your resume as this is also a space killer. Tables are charts for resumes that relay data for more senior level executives.

5. If your student has not had a paid position, internship, or job the heading should say "Volunteer Experience or Leadership Experience" if it applies to what will follow next. If your child has been a babysitter, the best term to use is caretaker as the position title. Use your imagination when talking about how awesome your student is. If they get awards all year long, they are locally recognized award winning....

6. If your student has a good GPA list it as an accomplishment. If your student has other things, they do such as volunteer at the shelter, your church, or community center list this as a position as well. Working is working regardless of pay or not. Your high schooler can show resilience in their professional career while showing a good range of community service assistance in the community.

7. Do not use text boxes or shapes on the resume when typing in your data. Some applicant tracking systems do not (parse) read the information in these shapes or boxes meaning all the information will disappear. If you add your contact details in a rectangle when it comes to the Recruiter all they will see is a blank space instead of the information you entered.

8. The most important rule is to remember resumes are living documents. When your student does something new please update their resume to reflect that new accomplishment. Did they receive a leadership award or volunteer of the year these words carry weight use them for the GREATER GOOD! I have furnished a current template I use for my high school clients. Nothing is written in stone, so feel free to

create "TRUTHFUL" content about your work or volunteer experience to make sure your teen gets the "Your hired" or "We want to extend an offer" conversation. If you have any questions while writing, please do not hesitate to reach out.

HIGH SCHOOL RESUME DRAFT

STUDENT NAME
Phone | Email Address | City, Florida Zip Code

EDUCATION

High School Sophomore | High School | City, State

Cultured honor roll sophomore proficient with unsupervised task execution, problem solving and follow up due to leadership training and experience from JROTC.
Adept with group or one on one interactions in a customer service centric environment.

(example of what this section could sound like for your son/daughter)

PROFESSIONAL EXPERIENCE

Volunteer Organization   From - To
High School   City, State
- Assisted with crowd control with entrancing and exiting at school sponsored sporting events.
- Ensured donated items with Toys for Tots were sorted and labeled according to organization specifications prior to distribution.
- Packaged nonperishable items for distribution at various community service events.

Job Title   From – To
Company Name   City, State
- Inspected perishable goods to be discarded to prevent selling or distributing expired foods.
- Created donation boxes for incoming food insecure shoppers to purchase.
- Discarded expired or outdated can goods and other food items while cleaning up the workstation prior to shift end.

Police Explorer   From – To
Company Name   City, State
- Operated various check points at private events to ensure patrons were given clear direction of travel routes to and from the event.
- Prevented auto theft and theft of personal belongings by completing on ground patrol of parking lots.
- Reported suspicious activity to the Commanding Officer ensuring patrons remained safe during events.

Team Player | Quick Learner | Concise Communication | Dedication | Honest | Reliable

(The content of the resume should be used as a guide of the types of sentences your student could create on their personal resume)

HUMAN VOICE COVER LETTER EXAMPLE

July 1, 2020 (change date every time you send)

Person name you are submitting or interviewing with
Company name
Company Address

RE: Career Opportunity- (title you are interviewing for)

Dear Person (you are interviewing with),

Your (position you are applying for) is a perfect fit for me, as I am a (what type of person are you?) that knows how to soft skill, soft skill, and soft skill.

Why Did I Pursue This Position?
It is personal for me. I love (what ever you get to do if hired in this position). I am a (soft skill) that naturally uses (soft skills) to create out the box solutions to situations. As a (name of the job you are applying for) my greatest success is building towards an organized and cohesive work environment.

Why Do I Want to Work for (enter the company name)?
Simply put... ever changing technology. At (company name) serving as an (name of the job) gives me the ability to create solutions for (company name) that will build my professional knowledge and skills. My goal is growth while learning more about (company name).

How Do I Fit In?
- With my life experience, I understand (things you know about the employer) brings an in-depth understanding of diversity and how to motivate persons of different backgrounds and cultures in ethical competition.
- I am ready to jump in heart first with my eyes and ears open to absorb from coworkers and leadership.

Let's Meet.
I am confident that, as you read my resume and recommendations on LinkedIn, you will determine that my qualifications, education, and commitment will make a difference at (company name). I would welcome the opportunity to discuss my submission. I look forward to meeting with you soon virtually or in person to answer any questions you may have.

Kind Regards,

First and Last Name

The next step you can utilize to help your teen find employment is create a positive social media presence for them. LinkedIn is an online platform where professionals post, network, and interact about various topics including employment opportunities. Linke-dIn is a great way to highlight your young professional to the mass-es. The reality is that LinkedIn, Glassdoor, and Indeed are heavily utilized to find employment, your teen will have to be diligent in their efforts to get noticed by HR professionals and Talent Acquisi-tion Managers.

Creating their profile is simple. Does your teen have Facebook, In-stagram, TikTok and Twitter? They would use those same steps to create their profile on LinkedIn. Upload a picture and create a compelling, telling, and eye catching about me section. With all this creativity flowing, be TRUTHFUL! Do not my embellish or create alternative facts about what your student has accomplished truth never returns void! The employer or hiring manager can smell the "smoke and mirrors" a mile away.

Your teen can also search for employment at the below mentioned link of Teen Hire (*https://www.hireteen.com/jobs/?q&l=tampa&age=16*). Teen hire is a search engine created specifically for a younger work-er. Searching for employment is a job, so I always suggest my high school clients search for employment Tuesday through Thursday leaving Monday and Friday as free time. You do not want to burn the candle at both ends. I believe searching for a job five days a week is a bit much and would be a chore you would eventually loathe.

So now that we have discussed all things transition the only thing left to do is conclude this chapter of life and welcome you and your teen to their next step.

THE CONCLUSION

At the conclusion of this book, I dare not forget to mention my sincere

gratitude for your purchase and time invested in reading until the end. As a single mother raising a son, I understand the concerns of making all the "right decisions" and applaud you for your continued dedication to your teen and their success. Our children are our futures and we as adults play a major part in it.

My motivation for everything I have completed as a person since 2002 has been my son Darvin Omari Harris. My introverted sunshine motivates me to consistently evaluate my steps in life as I know he is always quietly watching.

I CHOSE MY LEGACY

The statistic that I was labeled at birth, "a nothing" or "not so hot something" by my Father's mother, my grandmother Geneva"Betty"Russell. She spoke words one would never expect to hear from a loved one. Geneva's words echoed in my heart and gave me the fuel to drive this car called life. I eventually forgave my grandmother for the ill words. My grandmother spoke out of a deep rooted fear of failure for my teen parents as they were unwed and uneducated. She assumed that my birth would result in my Father, her son's failure in life. He would be forced to make decisions between his own education and the needs of being a father to three little girls. The anger and resentment of my grandmother drove my life for over 20 years. The way she made me question my own existence. I was determined to prove that I was the best mistake my Mother and Father ever made together.

Resources

https://www.theatlantic.com/education/archive/2016/01/where-are-all-the-high-school-grads-going/423285/

https://www.theclassroom.com/percentage-high-school-students-attend-college-after-graduation-1423.html

https://www.bls.gov/news.release/hsgec.nr0.htm

https://www.insider.com/27-great-schools-that-dont-require-sat-or-act-scores-2019-7#1the-university-of-chicago-does-not-require-sat-or-act-scores-27

US News article *https://www.usnews.com/education/scholarship-search-insider/articles/2018-03-15/7-types-of-scholarships-that-can-help-pay-for-college-graduate-school*

https://www.propertycasualty360.com/2019/09/24/how-your-car-insurance-rate-is-determined/?slreturn=20201027103927

https://www.rwm.org/trade-school-careers/

https://www.dictionary.com/browse/internship

http://www.fldoe.org/academics/career-adult-edu/apprenticeship-programs/pre-apprenticeship.stml

https://www.forbes.com/sites/susanadams/2015/01/30/the-10-best-websites-for-finding-an-internship/#13f5fe771b44

http://www.idealist.org/

CPSIA information can be obtained
at www.ICGtesting.com
Printed in the USA
LVHW051046030621
689239LV00016B/2246

9 781638 215776